SIKH MARTYRS

SIKH MARTYRS

BHAGAT LAKSHMAN SINGH

GYAN

Published by

GYAN

Gyan Publishing House
5, Ansari Road
Daryaganj, New Delhi-110002
Phone: 011-47034999, 9811692060
E-mail: books@gyanbooks.com

Distribution Network
gyanbooks.com
India, USA, Canada, UK, Australia

ISBN: 978-93-7225-746-5 (HB)

First Published, 1923

2nd Impression 2025

Printed at: Gyan Press, Delhi.

SIKH MARTYRS

Author: BHAGAT LAKSHMAN SINGH

SIKH MARTYRS

BY

BHAGAT LAKSHMAN SINGH

Late of the Provincial Educational Service :
Formerly Professor of History and Literature,
Gordon Misson College, Rawalpindi :
One of the Original
Promoters of the Khalsa College, Amritsar :
Editor of the
"Khalsa," the first English Organ of the Sikhs :
Author of the
"Life of Guru Govind Singh," in English, etc.

LAHORE BOOK SHOP
Clock Tower, LUDHIANA

FOREWORD

I feel diffident in writing a Foreword to the story of martyrs told with such refreshing vigour by my friend, Bhagat Lakshman Singh. The author is still animated by influences which operated in his boyhood, and when it was a fashion to ridicule miracles ; his stories deal with objective side mostly as mirrored in the minds of men who chronicled the events. He has not attempted to lift the veil from subjective mysteries. The Gurus, and men in whose hearts God dwelt, suffered no tortures; the *Atman* while still dwelling in the body could short-circuit the senses which transmitted pain, and remain in a state of bliss - *Sat-Chit-Anand*. The Gurus suffered martyrdom to point out the path of immortality and the unconquerable nature of the soul; and also to batter down the barriers that closed the sluices of sympathy and allowed hate to prevail in the hearts of men entrusted with authority. The remarkable part, as the story of Sikh Martyrs unfolds itself, is the absence of any expression of ill-will towards their tormentors by the tormented. The songs of praise which they chanted, when free, are poured forth in moments of apparent agony in an unending melody. Their message lingers— a source of inspiration and strength that knows no change—flowing eternally from the heart of God Himself.

The author deserves our thanks and congratulations; he could not have chosen a more inspiring subject, nor handled it in a better style, his descriptions produce visions of Divineful personalities, set upon a golden thread.

The agony and the sacrifice and the need of it is traced clearly by the author. I have merely supplemented his reflections by pointing out that where God dwells, there cannot be any consciousness of sacrifice. Humanity needs martyrs who refuse to accept injustice, selfishness, stupidity, and moral ugliness; who give their lives to set free the Divine attributes of love, goodness, wisdom and beauty.

JOGINDRA SINGH

IQBALNAGAR, N.W.R.
4th June, 1923

CONTENTS

INTRODUCTION

Ages had passed since the star of Brahmarishi Desh[1] became occult. No light was shed from the firmament, and in the pitch darkness that then reigned supreme, the Yavans danced merrily, holding aloft the bleeding heads of infant Rishi Kumars, and the wails and cries of Aryan mothers supplied the music. On one such occasion,[2] Guru Nanak himself was made captive, together with his bard, Mardana. The harrowing scene he witnessed has been graphically described by him in the Ad Granth, Rag Asa. The following is a free translation of a few lines from its two hymns:—

1. The tresses that adorned the heads, and which vermilion parted, are now cut by shears, and dust hideth the necks whose seductive look had enthralled many a heart.

1. Ancient name of the Punjab.
2. Massacre and plunder of Saidpur (Eminabad)

Ladies used to living in palaces know not where to lay their heads.

On the day they were married, their bridegrooms looked so handsome beside them.

They were brought home in palanquins, carved with ivory.

Scents were sprinkled on them, and light shone from their shining garments.

A lac of rupees was presented to them on their first entry into their new home, and another lac when they stood to take up the duties of their new position.

Coconuts and raisins were among the fruits that were served on their table, and they lent charm to the sofas they reclined on.

(Now) They are dragged with cords round their necks, and their pearl necklaces break.

Wealth and beauty that had brought them happiness, now turn enemies.

In obedience to their orders, the minions of the invader disgrace them and carry them off.

If people had given a thought to the future,

why should they have been reduced to such a plight ?

The Princes of India have lost their heads in the pursuit of love and pleasure.

Devastation and desolation follow the wake of Babar.

And babies have no mothers to feed them.

Mussalmans are not allowed time to pray and the Hindus to worship.

Men, who had neglected to remember Rama, are now refused the choice even of professing faith in Khuda.

Those who had fled return to their lodgings and enquire about the dear ones they had left behind.

They find them not, and congregate to lament and cry.

2. Where are the prancing steeds in the wilds and forests, and where the sounds of horns and bugles ?

Where are the armoured cars and the red liveries ?

Where are the looking glasses and enchanting faces ?

Where are the gates, mansions and palaces and where the pretentious inns ?

Where are the soft beds and charming damsels at whose sight sleep vanished ?

Where are the Pan (betel) leaves and Pan-sellers, and the damsels with lips red like rubies ? All have vanished from view !

It is this wealth that hath brought so much suffering. It is this wealth that hath caused so much loss.

Without sins wealth accumulateth not, and it beareth not company when one dieth.

Countless Pirs endeavoured to stop the Mir's progress, when they heard of his march against them ; but he came undaunted.

Private mansions and public buildings were set on fire, and children cried as they were flayed alive.

(Yet) no Mughal became blind. The incantations of the Pirs evidently did not prove efficacious

In the contest between the Mughals and the

Pathans, the former used powerful guns, and the latter brought furious war elephants;
But the Indians had forfeited the Creator's sympathy, and they had to expiate their sins by dying as they did.
Of Hindu Turk, Bhatti and Thakur women, veiled from head to foot,
Some are carried off, while others seek rest on the funeral ground.
How can they pass their nights in peace whose dear ones do not return home ?
The Lord doth all this Himself or through His agents. To whom should one complain?
Sorrow and joy come, as wilt by Thee, O Lord ! Where is one to go and cry ?
The Master is pleased when He seeth His orders carried out.

Sayeth Nanak, One receiveth what is ordained for him.

Such is the testimony borne by one whose name no one will take lightly, and whose statements not even the most bigoted of Turks* or their

*The word 'Turk' in this book is used promiscuously to denote Mussalmans of all races and denominations.

sans will dare controvert. We can easily gather from this account that the invading Mughals were most savage in their treatment of our people, that no discriminating treatment was accorded to the Punjabi Mussalmans who suffered equally with their Hindu countrymen, and that the Guru believed that for much of their suffering the Indians themselves were responsible on account of the self-indulgent, self-seeking lives they led. We further learn that the Sayads and the Brahmans were all sunk in superstition and that instead of presenting a united front to the common enemy and warding off the blow, they wasted their opportunity by seeking the aid of charms and amulets. The result was simply disastrous. For several days, Saidpur was in the hands of the marauding hosts. The horrors enacted naturally pained Guru Nanak. He had already started his mission of peace and good-will to all mankind. He now saw that this peace and good-will were impossible, until and unless people were freed from the tyrannic yoke of the reigning Turks, and the spiritual subjection of the Brahmans and their kindred sacts of itinerant preachers, such as Yogis and Sanyasis, who had failed to impart true knowledge and insist on the observance of the rules of right conduct, the transgression of which had brought Divine wrath on the people. To secure this two-fold object, he commenced a bold attack on the strongholds of the ruling orthodoxy. He does not appear to have started a regular agitation against Turk supremacy; perhaps, because he did not feel himself equal to the task, or because he believed, and truly so, that the political upheaval of the people would automatically follow their moral and spiritual uplift, as it eventually did, and as it will always do under similar conditions. His deep and versatile learning and persuasive eloquence were marvellous, and the life he led was so simple, so pure and so selfless that it did not take him long to establish a sort of Theocracy, the basic principle of which was the Fatherhood of God and the Brotherhood of man, with Baba Nanak as Guru, who taught the worship of one great God that wished all His creatures well and at whose gate all were welcome, despite the bars placed in the way of the less gifted people by an interested hierarchy provided, of course, they sought Him with the eye of true faith, and undertook to lead lives of trustful obedience.

A gospel such as this was naturally hailed by all the suffering and the woe-begone who had been kept down for ages past. The successors of Guru Nanak faithfully following in his wake, carried on their compaign against the old order of things, and matters reached their climax when Guru Govind Singh, the last and most powerful of Guru Nanak's successors, gave quite a distinctive colour to the Sikh church, which thenceforward had its own laws and its own ceremonies and rituals. The priestly classes, whom this change principally affected, were not indifferent spectators of this, as it seemed to them, heretical and subversive movement. They were too shrewd to willingly allow it to take root. So from the very first they took measures to meet their assailants and check their progress But, as says Turtullian, one of the early Christian evangelists, "the blood of the martyrs is the seed of the church." The greater the persecution, the more was the strength that was infused into the Sikh church. And when men began to take the lives of the Sikhs for their offence of asserting their birth-right to all-round freedom, and lay wáste their hearths and homes, that day was the day of *actual truimph of the Sikh cause. Men stood* aghast at the sight of the horrors enacted before their very eyes. Their hearts went over to the brave men who gladly gave their lives, in order that their brothers should live as self-reliant, self-respecting and sacrificing men. And time soon came when this wave of sympathy spread over the whole country and fresh recruits swarmed round the banner of the Sikh church, and took up the cross in their turn.

Men have been and are mostly conservative all over the world. In religion, particularly, they are averse to all change. The belief prevails that it is a sin to chànge the religion inherited from one's forefeathers. No one looks back with wistful eyes on the rude huts of his ancestors, their savage garments, coarse food and barbarous environments. The services of all arts and sciences are brought into requisition to get all imaginable comforts for the physical body. But the slightest deviation from the old ruts in the domain of religion, provokes the ire of both the learned and the unlearned. Even when there is a desire for change on the part of the people, there are classes who are interested in keeping them in check. The exaggerated importance given to the priestly hierarchy, the sancity attaching to their office, and the intrinsic value of their preferments, tempt them to acts of violence and repression; and, leagued with despots and tyrants, who, for similar reasons, have an interest in keeping mankind in bondage, they subject persons of unorthodox beliefs and ways to all conceivable torture. But no amount of physical suffering can shake the faith of true believers, and the more they are persecuted, the more their cause triumphs.

People may not believe in dogmatic Christianity, but it is impossible not to admire the unflinching courage and fortitude with which hundreds and thousands of Christian marytrs chose to bear suffering rather than renounce their faith in Lord Jesus. All the resources of the Roman Empire, under the Emperors of the type of the hated Nero, failed to shake the belief of the early Christians in the simple teachings of their Saviour. Henry VIII of England, and his daughter, Mary, condemned hundreds of noble Englishmen to be burnt at the stake. The Court of Inquisition committed thousands of people to the flames in Spain and Portugal. Whole provinces, peopled by the Waldness and Albigenses in France, were devastated and the population butchered by the order of the Pope; but the Huguenots refused to conform to the Romish creed. Christian women were violated by Christian soldiers, children were taken off the breasts of their mothers and dashed to pieces before their very eyes. But all these barbarous atrocities ultimately resulted in the complete overthrow of the unlimited power, which religious and political despots possessed, over the lives and properties of men. The great mass of humanity witnessed the sweet resignation, with which the martyrs bore all their suffering, and were touched. They felt the power of the soul-elevating reformed creed and were soon converted to it. From that time dates the freedom of human mind in Chirstendom.

It those same days when John Knox in Great Britain, Calvin in France and Luther in Germany, were engaged in tearing open the web of mysticism and superstition, which the Church functionaries had woven to entangle the ignorant masses, the Sikh Gurus in India were one after the other, fearlessly exposing the absurdities of the sanctified meshes, dignified as codes of religion, in which an extremely abject position was assigned to all classes of men below the ranks of the warrior and the priest, which legalized the eternal subordination of all non-Brahmans and non-Kshatryas, and which ordained that burning molten lead should be poured into the ears of Sudra, if he dared to hear a Vedic Mantra recited.

The believers in the old Brahmanical creeds were not so powerful in the Punjab as in the other parts of India. This deficiency the wily opponents of reform made up by exciting bad blood between the Government of the day and the heads of the Sikh Church. At first the opposition was not so pronounced. The holy Nanak was dismissed with the contemptuous appellation of "Kurahi," that is, heretic. His three immediate successors do not appear to have met very serious opposition. But, when Guru Arjan gave the Sikhs a scripture of their own, a campaign of virulent calumny was started to poison the ears of the Mughal Emperors and his lieutenants in the Punjab. The ties of comparative good-will between the Mussalmans and the Sikhs were severely strained and at last, in the time of the last two Gurus, they gave way and snaped. The Sikhs completely forgot the terrible persecution, which they had suffered at the hands of their own Hindu kith and kin, and came to regard the reigning Turk as the author of all their ills, whose power it was to them an act of merit to resist. It was not being exercised for the good of anybody, and it was meet and proper that it should go[1]

Thus, the same drama was being enacted in Asia and Europe at the same time. The lust for power, hallowed by time and tradition, had deadened all sense of responsibility in the men of higher classes. The lower orders of Indian humanity had lost all sense of self-respect. They were used as beasts of burden but they believed that their lot was God-ordained and hence unchangeable. Their wòmen were ravished ; but they took this to be an honour. Their earnings were taken away from them by various stratagems ; but they believed that they would get them back a thousand-fold in the other world They were purposely kept illiterate ; but they felt not their degradation.[2] The

1. These were the times of Aurangzeb, when the power of the Turks was gasping for breath, and of the later Mughal Emperors when it passed away.

2. A visit to the Kangra and Simla Hills would show this to be the case even now. No one can sit on the same cot with a Kanait. Gold ornaments cannot be worn by certain classes. A Rajput may take any number of concubines from any caste.

earth groaned under the weight of sin. It cried for a deliverer. The deliverer, nay deliverers, did come. What Calvin and Luther, Voltaire and Rousseu, Danton and Robespierre, did for the Reformation and the French Revolution in Europe, was done by Nanak and Govind Singh in Asia and India, and Kabir, Chaitanaya and Nam Dev in Northern India and Maharashtra; with this difference, however, that, while in Europe the great Teutonic princes were, at heart, jealous of the power of the Pope, whose bulls and interdicts had not unoften made them tremble on their thrones and who, therefore, took up the cause of the Reformation and contributed not a little towards its success, the apostles of the Reformation in India had to fight for their cause single-handed. The civil power lay in the hands of the alien conquering races whose professed Islam and who, therefore, did not much concern themselves with the religious quarrels of the conquered people. They were too deeply absorbed in their own immediate concerns to find time to think of the great problems that were swaying the minds of the more intelligent among the vast non-combatant depressed classes of thepopulation. They took no decisive step either to impede or to advance the great spiritual upheaval that was taking place under their nose and when they did interfere, it was in alliance with the hereditary high-placed reactionaries, both of the church and of the laity, unconscious of their kinship in beliefs with the professors of the new Gospel, and absolutely unaware of the risk they were incurring—the risk of complete self-destruction and self-effacement

It is a mistake to suppose, therefore, that the struggle of the Sikhs against the Mughals was a religious one, as uninformed persons would make people believe. There is, in fact, much that is common between Sikhism and Islam; nay, between all religious dispensations teaching the unity of God and the brotherhood of man. Mohammad took birth in a degenerate age among people, who were deeply sunk in gross sensuality and were cruelly apathetic and he strove to unite them by the ties of fellowship and common belicf. Likewise, Nanak, the founder of Sikhism, and Govind Singh, the founder of the Khalsa Dispensation, were ardent reformers, who warned people of the dangers of unbelief, and taught them to have boundless faith in on' common, living, loving, and love-inspiring Divinity, that pervaded all existence and loved to nurture and watch over all creation. The Mussalmans generally recognised this from the very birth of Sikhism. They claimed the first Guru as their own. Mussalman saints, like Hazrat Mian Mir, and Hazrat Farid, Mussalman emperors like Babar and Akbar, Mussalman princes like Dara Shikoh and Muazzam, all, felt and displayed a cordial liking for Guru Nanak's Gospel. Even in our own days, Mussalman Pirs and savants love to talk of Guru Nanak's mission in the most enthusiastic terms

Islam has done for India what Hinduism had never aimed at doing, and what even Sikhism has very considerably failed to accomplish under Hindu influence. Hinduism had, one is sorry to sav, little consolation to offer to the depressed classes. Converts to Islam from Hinduism were, however, more advantageously placed. Those who came within its fold were at once raised religiously, socially and politically. For such the advent of Islam has been an undoubted blessing. Moreover, the Mussalman Mullah has generally had no prejudice in the matter of education. He held his school in his own house or in the village mosque, to which children of all religious persuasions were equally welcome. Nay, he was like a father to them. It was to his own Mussalman teacher that Guru Govind Singh owed his escape from Machhiwara. Wherever there was a Mullah, there was an elementary school That is to say, Mussalman India was covered by a network of schools, where the rudiments of knowledge, such as it was then known, were ungrudgingly imparted. Thus Islam that, born in the arid wastes of Arabia, had called the light of knowledge to the homes of the Spaniards and the Portuguese, the Gaul and the Goth, the Roman and the Greek during the Dark Ages, exercised the same benignant influence in the great continent of India. It is unfortunate, very unfortunate, indeed, that believers in the unifying creed of Islam and those in the equally eclectic creed of Baba Nanak and the noble Guru Govind Singh, should have fallen out with one another and brought about untold misery upon themselves. Aurangzeb and, later on, the men to whom the Mughal power was transferred, were guilty of violence in their dealings with the subject people. Had these men been of a better calibre, had they been gifted with political wisdom and foresight they would have known that administrative mistakes, however, shall they might appear at the time of commission, become, in the end, store-houses of cordite, and that, sometimes, even a spark blows up great empires, and a small force scatters big hosts to the wind. "When one individual of a community," says the great seer Sa'di, "does an act of unwisdom, both the great and the small lose their dignity." Had Guru Arjan been generously treated, had Aurangzeb seen and known how wrong and useless it was to forcibly convert people to his creed, had he not cruelly put to death the saintly Guru Tegh Bahadur, had he, even when grown old and experienced in state-craft, seen through the machinations of the confederate Hindu Hill Rajahs of the Punjab, and abstained from molesting Guru Govind Singh, had Bazid Khan, Governor of Sirhind, been humane; and had he not bricked up alive the two infant sons of Guru Govind Singh — thousands and tens of thousands of Sikh and Mussalman lives would not have formed part of a big Punjabwide holocaust, and the successors of the idealist Nanak would have been free to devote their whole attention to their conquests in the domain of the spirit, which lay mainly unexploited, and for success in which only the weapons of love and persuasion were needed.

The Sikh Gurus, one and all, never valued the importance of lip-professions in religious creeds. Born in Hindu families, and belonging to the highest castes, that prided themselves on their ancient lineage and tenaciously held to their traditions, they have put it in black and white that only, the belief in one common Divine Father and obedience to His will are of avail. "The Hindu is blind, the Turk one-eyed," says the Guru. "Of the two, he is wiser who possesseth discernment." Bhai Gur Das Bhalla, who occupies the position of Saint Paul in Sikh history, lays in his immortal Vars (Psalms) that, when Baba Nanak visited Mecca, its priest asked him whether he believed the Hindus to be true or the Mussalmans. The Baba replied that he thought that without good deed both were doomed, and that the Pundits and the Mullahs were uselessly frittering away their energies in religious disputations.

This explains the attitude of Sikhism with respect to Islam and all other creeds of the world. All these creeds embody principles of right conduct, with some reservations here and there, dictated by the necessities of the times when they were first promulgated. Sikhism would tolerate any system of belief if it allowed freedom of worship and drew men closer to one another and to their common Divine Father. From Baba Nanak down to the illustrious Guru Govind Singh—all particularly emphasise this eclecticism in the matter of belief. In mountains and valleys, in rivers and riverine tracts, in seas and gulfs, in deserts and jungles, in arid wastes and gardens, in the sky and on the earth, in all stellar regions and the nether worlds, Guru Govind Singh sees, like the Qais of blessed memory, only his beloved Laila, his Father in Heaven, who dispenses all that is good and whose resplendent face sheds refulgence all over the world.

Patriorism after all, is a feeling of selfishness and narrow-mindedness. The Sikh Gurus, were not mere men – they were greater and nobler than angels The whole world was their home, and the wide universe their country. Guru Govind Singh saw God in all things, and he believed that that Turks, Arabs and Persians, Ladakhis, Chinese, Japanese, Bengalis, Rohillas and Khurasanis, Northerns, Southerns, Easterns and Westerns, Kandharis, Kureshis and Farangis – all – who had faith in God and His goodness, would thrive and blossom, like flowers in a well- kept garden. A man of such cosmopolitan sympathies, which even contemporary Mussalmans of note did not fail to recognise, and some of whom espoused his cause at marvellous self-sacrifice, could certainly have no quarrel with any well-disposed and God-fearing individual; and when even he felt compelled to resort to active resistance, we may safely assume that the state of things under the ruling classes of the time had become simply unbearable.

All living creation is engaged in an eternal death-struggle. The strong live upon the weak To escape absorption and extinction, it is absolutely necessary that the weak should become strong, and the strong should see that they be not lose their vitality and virility. What people call a life of peace is, at best, the life of the bovine species of creation who love to ruminate sheepishly, and who are constitutionally unfitted to conceive of subtle problems and attempt their solution. To chastise evil-doers and to face danger is the work of heroes, of gods,--not of the good people who float along like dead fish.

The dark lowering clouds spread over the

sky and envelop the land. At the sight of their menacing look, the craven-hearted animals conceal themselves in their holes. The fowls seek shelter in their nests, and the fish dive deep to escape from the buffeting of the surging waters above. Even the wolf and the hyena crouch in their dens. The thunder bursts forth and shakes the loftiest mountains, and the very earth shakes and trembles. The lightning rends asunder the tallest of trees The winds in their fury uproot even the gigantic oak and sweep off lofty turrets of great mansions. But the lion quails not. He views the dismal scene quite unconcernedly, and majestically walks along to his retreat—ready to fall upon his enemy, should he chance to meet one. Much more is expected from a self-respecting person. If there is anything which lends fascination and charm to an individual, it is his readiness to defend himself and those who look to him for help and protection, and to make it difficult for people, malevolently inclined, to molest them. Such a beauty can only be born of sincerity of belief and depth of conviction. Guru Govind Singh's aim was to create men with hearts like those of lions, with the faith and devotion of a Pathan Ghazi, whom nothing would tempt, who feared nobody, who wanted nothing, and, who, carrying their lives on the palms of their hands, would know no rest , till they had destroyed the power of the Evil One in the sacred Bharat. How far he succeeded in his aims, his record bears testimony to most eloquently.

The thick-headed Mughal has never been famous for the possession of gifts that could win him any one's esteem anywhere. His history is one long tale of barbarity and imbecility. Timur and Changez swept over Asia and Europe down to the very banks of the Danube, like a hurricane, leaving only marks of devastation behind. They consolidated no state and established no empire. If the maniac Nero played upon his fiddle when Rome burnt, Timur delighted in shooting at the minarets, made of the skulls of the innocent Punjabis, whom he carried off into slavery and slew at pleasure. Their descendant, Babar, was easily able to establish himself as the sovereign of northern India; but the dynasty, he founded, has left no mark or impress, which could remind one of the solicitude of the Mughal rulers for the people that had come to be placed under their charge. It produced no Naushirwan, no Vikramaditya, and no Asoka. What Sher Khan Suri could achieve, for public weal, during nine years of established rule, what the administrators of the British East India Company could accomplish, for the good of the people, during two decades of their sway, could not be done by the Mughals during centuries of their rule. They established no big school, no college or university, no hospital no well organized court of judicature. No river was bridged, no road was metalled. Every strong man, every where, was a ruler, and the lives and property of the people were at the mercy of every petty official. The chief anxiety of the various provincial governors was how to collect revenue, which they spent in drink and debauch, and a part of which they advisedly contributed for the expenses of the gay autocrat, who sat on the Delhi throne, and whom they loved to copy in every detail. One reign of the enlightened Akbar, who loved peace, whom gods favoured and men worshipped, whe was blessed with honest and faithful administrators like Bairam Khan, generals like Man Singh, financiers like Abul Fazal, and literati like Faizi, and whose age produced a man of Abul Qasam's fidelity, who gave his life to save his friend Bairam Khan, cannot redeem the wrongs of generations of Mughal misrule. It rather stands out as a flaring light, in a dark, dreary and tempestuous night, displaying its hideousness in bold relief.

Before the advent of the Mughals, India had Mussalman rulers. They were good, they were bad. There was Ala-ud-Din who waged wars to possess beautiful damsels. There was Kai Kubad, who loved to dance as a dancing girl. And there was Mohammad Tughlak who marched expeditions to the far-off China, without making adequate arrangements for supply and transport, and who transported the whole population of the Imperial Delhi to found a capital at Daulatabad in the Deccan. But there was also the emperor Nasir-ud-Din, who considered it unlawful to spend Imperial revenues on his own needs, who lived on the earnings of his own hands, and whose wife had to cook for him and for herself and go without a maid-servant. Even the greedy Mahmud of Ghazni could boast that he shared the plunders of India with his nobles and sardars. But the best Mughal rulers, with very few exceptions, sought their thrones and got them through fratricide. As for the others, the less said the better. They were mostly puppets, set up by ambitious ministers, or by the officers of the Imperial Guard, as was the case with most of the later Roman Emperors of the Eastern Byzantine Empire—not unlike whom they wielded no authority and exercised no control over what was going on in the provinces, of which they were the nominal rulers.

Of the many unbelievable stories, which disfigure the pages of the Sikh chronicles, and which make them of questionable historical value, is the one which attributes to Guru Nanak the blessing that Babar's descendants should rule over India for seven generations. Easily gullible though men generally are, it passes comprehension how it is believable that a high-souled person of Guru Nanak's purity of intention was capable of bearing even the sight of his people being governed by the Mughals, not to speak of his desiring the continuance of their rule, merely for the reason that Babar had released him from captivity on learning that he was a man of God. To my mind, individuals as well as nations are subject to the law of Karma. It was due to the misdeeds of their forefathers, who had practised unbearable atrocities on the aboriginal races of India, that the Indians of Aryan extraction were doomed to eternal subordination and came to be governed by the Mughals; when the country had practically ceased to have a ruler actuated by the desire, and possessed of the capacity; to rule with fear of God in his breast and love of fellow-men in his heart, and when spoliation and plunder, ravishing of women and condemning of people to death for slight offences or for no offence at all, had become matters of course.

The events I am about to record were typical examples of everyday occurrence. Men generally got accustomed to the state of things under which they lived, and either lost all feeling of shame and honour, or bore insult and molestation with patience and resignation. It is only where resistance was offered with success that public attention was attracted, and harrowing incidents of the sufferings entailed were remembered, and handed down to posterity from mouth to mouth, or formed the theme of song by national bards. The recording of these events during the time in which they occurred was unthinkable. The difficulty of preparing anything like a regular history may, therefore, be well imagined. After long travels and arduous labour the late Gyani Gyan Singh of Patiala wrote standard works on the subject a couple of decades ago. But they are in Punjabi and Urdu, and hence not intelligible to those who do not understand those languages. Mine is an humble effort to place in the hands of the reader an abbreviated volume written in a language which is most widely understood throughout the world, in the hope that a wider humanity may know something of the men who played so important a part in the world-drama and who sacrificed their lives for the uplift of their downtrodden fellow-beings.

The Sikh martyrs, by a magic wand, as it were, completely metamorphosed the society and the country that gave them birth. They completely changed the course of events in the times in which they lived, falsifying the much-talked-of and much commented-upon theory that great men are mere products of their times. Men looked upon them with awe and wonder. The Sikh name acquired a new significance and new dignity. Mighty Nawabs and great soldiers trembled at its very mention. The empire of the great Mughal was shaken to its very foundation by the first blow struck by the enraged Sikhs, immediately after the innocent children of the great Guru Govind Singh received martyrdom at Sirhind.

Men have died all the world over, while exploiting for land, wealth or woman, but the credit of dying for the weak and the oppressed, and for the upholding of Truth, belongs to the Christian and the Sikh martyrs alone The work done by Islam has been great. It rescued nations from a life of complete mental and moral degradation, and it has infused a wonderful love for one another in the believers. But it cannot be said that the men, who laid down their lives for it, were actuated altogether by pure motives. The promise was held out to them, and in this promise they believed with a tenacity of which Mussalmans alone are capable that they would get Houries and Ghilmans in the other world for the lives they gave in this. The Christian and the Sikh martyrs had no such temptation. The one ambition of the Christian martyr was to be born again through death, to live at the feet of his Lord and the only wish and hope of the Sikh matyr was to have an abode for his undying spirit in the 'Sach Khand,' the region of Truth, where he believed God lived, to look at Him and glorify Him ever and ever ! ! ! !

Saidpuri Gate
Rawal Pindi — LAKSHMAN SINGH
5th October, 1919

CHAPTER I

GURU ARJAN DEV

This first Sikh matyr was born on the 18th of Bisakh, Tuesday, 1610 Vik., according to 1554 A.D. He was the second son of Guru Ram Das, the first Guru of the Sodhi clan, that has played so noble a part in Sikh history. As a child he was so sweet, loving, humble and dutiful that his parents doted on him. These qualities he retained till the close of his earthly career. From his early years, he devoted himself to self-culture, and grew to be a man of great scholarship and piety. He was particularly fond of the company of ascetics of both the Hindu and Mussalman persuasions. Among the chief saints, with whom he had formed ties of attachment, were Hazart Mian Mir, whose remains are enshrined in the tomb close to the Lahore Cantonment, Shah Hussain, whose sublime and stirring hymns still apeal to so many pious people in our land, and Bhagat Chhajju, the famous Hindu saint of Lahore, whose simple and upright living people remember so admiringly, and whose place of abode is still visited as a shrine. But from his very childhood young Arjan had a mortal enemy in his elder brother, Prithi Chand, a haughty, greedy, intriguing, and unscrupulous person, who had conceived a dislike for him because of the special fondness which his parents showed to him. Prithi Chand feared lest this partiality for his younger brother might lean to his own claim to the *Gadi* (succession) being overlooked.

The fact was that the *Gadi* of the Sikh Gurus had by this time become a seat of might and influence, through the loving sympathy and magnanimity of Guru Ram Das. And it came about in this way. During one of his preaching tours, the Guru had halted at a secluded spot in the wilds Manjha. Close by was a pool of water, the sanctity of which had been demonstrated in a very remarkable manner.[1]

---

1. The story goes resembling in many details the well-known dramatic play of King Lear and his daughters, that Duni Chand, a jagirdar of Patti in the Lahore district, had five daughters. Once, when the father was also present, the four elder girls prided themselves on being the lucky daughters of an influential chief. The youngest observed that all affluence was due to God's grace, to whom alone was gratitude mostly due. This incensed the father who, forthwith, gave the youngest in marriage to a leaper, who was also a cripple. The girl received this treatment with calm resignation. From that time forward she carried her husband about in a basket on her head, and supported herself on public charity and on the roots and leaves of wild trees. Arriving at this pool, she took off her burden from her head, placed it on the ground and went to pay her obeisance to Guru Ram Das, who lay encamped in the vicinity. While she was away, the cripple observed a jackdaw dipping in the water and forth-with turning into a swan with snow-white feathers. He felt a strong desire to imitate the jackdaw. He dragged himself to the brink of the pool and throw himself into the water, when, wonder of wonders, his leprosy was forthwith healed and his limbs were made whole. When the wife returned, she wanted to know what had become of her crippled husband. The man explained the change. But she was not satisfied. The matter was at last reported to the Guru, who assured her that the man was her husband, and named the spot Dukh Bhanjni

The Guru enlarged this pool and laid on its bank the foundations of a splendid temple, which took several generations to complete. He also built here a house for his own residence, and quarters for the reception of visitors. Round this group of buildings sprang a large town which, at the present time, is the most populous and wealthy in the province, being the premier seat of sikh pilgrimage and central market for trade. Guru Ram Das was, moreover, a model benefector. The poor and the needy found in him a generous patron, and the rich loved to honour him. In fact, all sections of the community looked up to him for advice in matters worldly and spiritual.

His elder son, Prithi Chand, shrewd as he was, saw the growing influence of the place and, therefore, felt very much annoyed when he noticed his father's partiality for the young Arjan. He, accordingly intrigued with the Mussalman Governor of Lahore for the removal of his youngest brother from Amritsar. The plot

---

(Reliever of Pain), and called the pool 'Amritsar' (the Tank of Immortality).

does not appear to have succeeded and Arjan continued to reside in Amritsar. A small incident, however, soon developed into a serious quarrel between the father and the son. Lahori Mal, a cousin of Guru Arjan Dev was to be married at Lahore. The Guru was invited to attend with his wife and sons. Prithi Chand was requested to go and represent the family; but he refused to comply. He felt it hard to leave, even for a while, the lucrative position of chief steward, that he held in the Guru's household, and Arjan Dev had to be sent instead. But this only precipitated the consequence of which Prithi Chand was so mightly afraid. Arjan Dev was not only a son to the Guru he was his counterpart. To live away from his father was to him as good as death. He had not been long in Lahore before he began to send to his father epistle after epistle, showing how disconsolate he had become and how he yearned to return. These letters were intercepted by Prithi Chand. The fact came to the knowledge of the Guru. A search being made, the letters were found on the person of Prithi

Chand. The Guru was naturally incensed. He forthwith sent for Arjan Dev, and in order to to prevent internecine feuds afterwards, he was anointed as successor to the *Gadi* then and there. But this was by no means the end of the matter, as will subsequently appear.

The succession of Guru Arjan Dev to the *Gadi* was the introduction of a new era in the history of Sikhism. His manifold activities infused public spirit into the community. Places of worship were built wherever Sikh influence was felt. Large tanks were dug and lands were set apart, the proceeds of which went to defray the expenses of their upkeep. Men took pleasure in succouring those in need. Each well-to-do individual was a banker to the community and he advanced money at a nominal rate of interest, perfectly sure that his money was safe. The practice of requiring written or sealed bonds from the creditors was unknown, and community showed signs of affluence that it had never before known. Another remarkable achievement of the Guru was the compilation of the Granth, The Sikh Bible. The writings of the previous Gurus had been preserved on stray scraps of paper stitched together. The Guru consolidated them in chronological order and set them to the sublimest music then known. He incorporated into the volume a number of hymns composed by Hindu and Mussalman saints, who had striven to lead a life of godliness and had thus set the highest and noblest example of right living to their fellow-beings. This was an example of catholicity, quite unique. Men remember it with a feeling of pride now. But in the Guru's time they thought differently. The Sikhs, of course, submitted deferentially to whatever the Guru did It was the orthodox Hindu priests who took umbrage at this. To them the idea of compiling a scripture in a language other than Sanskrit or Hindi and the inclusion therein of the word of low-caste Hindus or Mussalmans, was exceedingly abhorrent. The effort to organize the Sikh dissenters into a strong commonwealth, which aimed at casting off the irksome influence of many time-honoured institutions, spread a feeling of alarm throughout the orthodox circles. The leaders had recourse to the usual tactics in discrediting the Sikh propaganda. Failing in this, they represented to the rulers of the day that the Guru was preaching a revolt against the paramount power, and that the Granth he had compiled contained references derogatory to the founder of Islam. Prithi Chand heard this opposition. Through the good offices of Wazir Khan, Subah of Lahore, who admired the Guru as a man of God, this effort to discredit him and invite suspicion against his propaganda failed But quite an unforeseen circumstance strengthened the cause of the Guru's opponents and led to his incarceration and death by extreme torture.

Jehangir's son, Khusro, rebelled against his father. Failing in his efforts to win popular sympathy for his cause, he fled to the Punjab. The Guru was the only man of note in the province. The prince took shelter with the Guru, who received him cordially. The Guru knew that he was thus giving mortal offence to Jehangir. He also knew what capital his oppenents in the province would make out of this act. The die was, however, cast and there was no help for it. The law of hospitality was hard to break, especially by a successor of Guru Nanak. He had to use his own discretion and stake his all, regardless of the people's praise or dispraise, approval or disapproval. When Prince Khusro thought he should leave the Guru's protection, he applied to him for financial assistance which was readily granted. The hapless prince was however soon arrested and deprived of his eyesight.

The behaviour of the Guru infuriated Jehangir and he lost no time in taking his revenge. This is how he writes of the Guru in his memoirs:—
' So many of the simple-minded Hindus, nay many foolish Moslems, too, had been fascinated by his ways and teachings. He was noised about as a great religious and worldly leader. They called him Guru, and from all directions crowds of people would come to him and express great devotion to him This busy traffic had been carried on for three or four generations. For many years the thought had presented itself to my mind that either I should put an end to this

false traffic or that *he should be brought within the pale of Islam* " The pious wish expressed in the italicised words was, however, not carried out, presumably because personal factor had now come in. A harder treatment was now thought necessary. He did not impale the Guru alive, as he did in the case of Khusro's companions He thought it more politic to impose a heavy fine on the Guru, and placed him in the custody of Chandu Lal a powerful Hindu minister at the Lahore Court, who had become the Guru's bitter enemy on account of the latter's refusal to betrothe his son, Har Govind, to Chandu's daughter. The torments that the Guru suffered at the hands of this infamous miscreant are difficult to describe. Blood freezes in the veins at the very thought of them. The Guru lay confined in a cell below the compartments occupied by Chandu. Here Chandu would approach the Guru daily to press his old suit. At other times, he would ask him to insert valedictory hymns in praise of the Prophet Mohammad in the Granth Sahib, in consideration for which he would have the

Guru's life spared. Neither of these requests could be complied with. Guru Nanak's was not the house for a marriage by force. And the Granth Sahib contained only the praise of God. No mortal man's praise finds room in its pages. True, there are a few verses in it in praise of Guru Nanak; but no Guru has written anything else in it but the praise of the One Great Lord. In a word, when Chandu knew that there was no hope of the Guru giving way, he ordered hot burning sand to be poured on the Guru's body. Not content with this, he made him sit on a red-hot iron plate. These inhuman tortures could not last long. The Guru soon gave up his ghost (1606 A.D.) and his remains were thrown into the Ravi which then flowed at the foot of the walls of the fortress! On this spot now stands a handsome temple where an annual fair takes place.[1]

1. According to another tradition, it was decided to sew the Guru in the hide of a cow. When everything was ready, the Guru asked permission to bathe in the Ravi. He was sent there with a strong escort, but having once plunged into the running water, he never appeared again. (See Mohammad Latif's History of the Punjab, page 254).

Chandu did not escape chastisement for his wicked deeds. The fickle Foitune forsook him before the lapse of many years, when the martyred Guru's son and successor, Guru Har Govind, had him arrested and put to death.

There is a touching story of the great love in which the Moslem saint, Hazrat Mian Mir, held the Guru. It is said that the saint came to see the Guru during the oays of his incarceration, and was struck with horror at the sight of the inhuman tortures to which the Guru was being subjected. He showered imprecations on Jehangir's head and asked the Guru for permission to pray for the overthrow of the Mughal rule. But the Guru would not consent to such a course. He said he would resignedly leave himself in the hands of God, who alone knew what was good. And the Guru was right. Whatever dignity or nobility attaches to the name Sikh, is primarily due to this one of the most unostentatious, quotest and humblest of workers in the cause of Truth.

CHAPTER II

GURU TEGH BAHADUR

This is the second of the great Sodhi Gurus who received martyrdom (1675 A.D.) The readers of history cannot be unaware of the persecution of the Hindus in the time of Aurangzeb. The Sikhs then, as now, were identified with the Hindus to all intents and purposes. From the time of the unlucky Jai Pal down to the days of Baba Nanak, the Hindus of the Punjab had no leader to whom they could appeal for help. For full four centuries, they had lived as outlaws in their own country. Their lives and property were always unsafe at the disposal of the Mussalmans. Mussalmans forcibly carried off Hindu girls for immoral purposes, but there was no appeal. Nanak's heart bled at the thought of Turk-oppression. Says he :-

"The age is of knife, and rules are butches.

Virtue hath taken wings and fled.

The dark night of Amavas hath enveloped the moon of Truth.

And men look for her reappearance in vain."

Thus it was given to Baba Nanak to truly see the plight of the down-trodden Hindus, and to devise means for its amelioration. He taught his people right thinking and right living, and made them self-respecting and self-reliant. They became devout people, indifferent to outward glitter. Their wants were simple and, therefore, they had leisure enough to think of the higher problems of life. So, wherever there was a Sikh; there was life. The Guru and his successors came to be regarded as the source of all wisdom and all power. They came to be known and remembered as Sacha Padshahs. True king;—in contradistinction to the kings that had away over temporal things; and rightly so. For what; after all; have our so-called kings to give to anybody ? If it is true, as says Shakespeare, that ' uneasy lies the head that wears a crown," what ease can such heads give to those who depend on them ? Say what political conjured may, they cannot hide from themselves the fact that it is their thirst for pelf and power that prompts them to do the deeds that they so innocently call great. Such is not the case with men of God, as the Sikh Gurus were. People looked up to them for help as a nursling clings to the breast of its mother. Who can count the number of mothers that have jumped out of running railway trains to pick up their infants, who had fallen from their protecting arms, or the number of mothers that have jumped into tempestuous torrents to rescue their drowning children, disregardful of risk to themselves ? How many mothers have sacrificed their own lives in order that their young ones should live ! The Sikh Gurus were mothers to their people, so to say. They were not self-contained, self-centred men, given to indulgence in spiritual charlatanism and chicanery, which appeal so much to the gullible humanity all the world over. They were all practical men of action who believed more in dead than in word, and whose heart and soul were wholly devoted to the well-being of their fellowmen. No wonder, therefore, if for this reason, they should have come to be regarded by the Hindu population as their Sacha Padshahs, who, in their turn, defended them from internal and external trouble.

It was some such feeling as this which prompted the Brahmans of Kashmir to wait upon the 9th Guru and seek his aid against Mughal oppression. How in those days, under instructions from Aurangzeb, a campaign had been started to convert the weak, nerveless Kashmiri Hindus to Islam is a matter of history. I have described it at some length in my "Life of Guru Gobind Singh". For the present narrative it will suffice to say that in Srinagar alone, thousands of Hindus were forcibly made Mussalmans. Elsewhere I have given an expression to my own views on the relative importance of the different religious creeds. and I have there stated that to my mind the Moslem creed is decidedly nobler and more acceptable to a self-respecting, virile, people than the numerous Hindu creeds, believed in by the bulk of the Indian population, that teach man-worship and idol-worship and inculcate gross sensualities. But men, all the world over, particularly when they have lived amid civilized surroundings, come to have naturally quite a sort of partiality for the opinions which they inherit from their ancestors. They come to feel a sort of pride in the views they hold, specially religious views, and they would rather give their lives than be converted to a new creed. This is all the more so when the new creed belongs to their hated alien oppressors, who rob them of all that men hold dear. In the Punjab specially, the state of things had become acute. Here for about two centuries, men had heard the sublime teaching of the great Guru Nanak and his equally great successors, and their hearts had begun to pulsate with newer emotions and their minds to be imbued with chastened ideas that enabled them to take a higher view of existence and taught them to feel a real and abiding interest in their fellowmen-

For the first time a great province of the Indian continent had begun to be swayed by the feeling of nationality. Men of all castes and ranks had been united by the ties of brotherhood which, under the galvanizing influence of the Gurus, had come to possess a potentiality that had to be reckoned with. The followers of this leader could on no account be made to see much beauty in the foreign creed, professed by the Turks. Naturally, when an attempt was made to forcibly convert their Hindu kith and kin, a feeling of anguish passed through their whole frame.

But I am digressing a bit, I am afraid. Guru Tegh Bahadur, we can easily suppose, must have felt deeply distressed on hearing the tale of woe told by the deputation of the Kashmir Brahmans. And we can imagine how deeply he must have felt the necessity for doing something effective to ease the situation. But he was powerless to offer any active resistance. His father, Guru Har Govind, always had a small band of soldiers with him, and on a few occasions he actually fought battles with the Imperial forces. But it does not appear from the contemporary chronicles that Guru Tegh Bahadur ever gave a thought to train his men for a military career. How he came to have the name of Tegh Bahadur—Hero of the Sword—is more than I can say. All accounts agree in his having lived the life of a recluse in the village of Bakala, in the Amritsar district, before he was called upon to occupy Guru Nank's *Gadi*, at a very advanced age. Indeed the writings that he has left, which thanks to the boldness of his illustrious son and successor, Guru Govind Singh, adorn the pages of the Ad Granth, are all couched in the style of the early Buddhist saints and the later Hindu Bhagats, who emphasize the emphemeral nature of all worldly ries and connections and thc reality only of living in spirit, living in the Lord. The only expedition in which he had a share was the one which took him to Assam. But the only part he appears to have taken in this was to obtain for the Assam prince an honourable peace. So there was no inconsistency in the attitude of the Guru. He was, all along, a lover of peace and quiet. The only way open to him, therefore, was to proceed to Delhi and personally protest against Aurangzeb's policy of forcing people to change their religious beliefs. This he did. In this step he was encouraged by has only son, Govind Rai (the future Guru Govind Singh); who was then a mere lad of eight years. When the Guru observed to the deputation that the situation could be eased only if a noble soul offered himself as a sacrifice at the altar of his country, the brave Govind Rai at once stood up, placed his arms round the Guru's neck and lovingly said, "Father dear, who could be nobler than thee and fitter for such an honourable deed ?" This was enough. The Guru's decision was made, and he lost no time in giving effect to it. Accompanied by half-a-dozen followers, he proceeded to Delhi; but before he could arrange a meeting with the emperor, the latter's over-zealous officers arrested him at a garden in Agra and took him to Delhi, where he was incarcerated in a common jail. When, at last he was brought before Aurangzeb, the bigoted Mughal is said to have used all his power to persuade him to accept the creed of Islam, under the belief that the Guru's conversion would bring large numbers of the Punjab Hindus in the fold of Islam. But all his attempts were in vain. Upon this, the wily emperor who had waded to the throne through the blood of his brothers, true to his instincts, first ordered the Guru's companions, Bhais Mati Das and Dayal Chand to be tortured to death, which was done. The Guru himself was then slain and quartered and the fragments of his body were hung on the four gates of Delhi.[1] Cunning though he was, Aurangzeb lacked in imagination. He could not see the consequences of his cruelty and double-dealing, and this was the main reason why the kingdom that he had inherited and which his ancestors had ruled so long and consolidated, fell like a house of cards. It is needless to mention that before being put to death, the Guru was subjected to inhuman tortures. It was in those days when he was undergoing

1, The Guru's place of martyrdom bears the name of Sis Ganj and is situated in Chandni Chauk.

these sufferings, that the Guru wrote his famous 'Slokas" (verses), which were subsequently incorporated into the Granth Sahib by his illustrious son and successor. In these he describes in heart catching language the falsity of all worldly grandeur which, says he is as unstable as a wall of sand. Rama and Ravan who had such a large offspring have gone. The world is impermanent and unreal like a dream. Anxiety need only he felt for an unusual happening. All that takes birth passes away, some day or other. Hence he recommends freedom from worldly entanglements and singing instead the glories of the most High. This stage of mentality is a necessary condition before one can aspire to win the crown of martyrdom. All martyrs really belong to a higher and purer world to which they are every ready to go without fret or murmur. The "Slokas" also bear testimony to the well-known fact that when trouble comes, summer-day Friends show the white feather and turn away."Friends and companions", says the Guru,"have all parted company; none hath shown steadfastness. In this dire calamity, the Lord alone is my prop and stay." Once he writes to his son, that strength has failed him, he has been caught in a net and knows not how to get out, unless God, in his mercy, comes to his rescue. And the reply of Govind Rai is characteristic He refuses to believe that the Guru is serious in writing thus. Full well he knows that the Guru is an embodiment of all power and courage, too high for care and anxiety to touch him, and too resourceful to need a helper.

The Guru's illustrious great grandfather, the prince of saints, the most cultured man of the age, and yet the lowliest of the lowly, was the first to win the crown of martyrdom. The second to win this glorious distinction was he himself, the most renowned man of his age,—the simplest, meekest and most unassuming of men that were ever born. The inhuman treatment accorded to such a man was bound to provoke his people as nothing else could have done. His noble son and successor, Guru Govind Singh, speaks the bare truth when he says :-

The world went into mourning when Guru Tegh Bahadur departed.

Men on earth wailed and cried, and angels rejoiced in god-land.

Flowers were showered from the sky;

Congratulation poured in from all sides.

Glory to Thee, O, people's Monarch ! ! !

To the Chastiser of the vicious and the Elevator of the lowly ! ! !

CHAPTER III

BHAIS MATI DAS AND DAYAL CHAND

Reference has already been made to the martyrdom of Bhais Mati Das and Dayal Chand, who had accompanied the Guru on his fatal journey to Delhi, and had laid down their own lives for him. Bhai Mati Das was a Muihal Brahman of Kariala in the Jhelum district, about six miles from Chakwal on the road to Katas Raj, which is a well-known place of Hindu pilgrimage, noted for its natural beauty The village is situated on the spurs of the Surla Mountains amidst very inspiring surroundings. The part of the country is known as Dhani, which means rich. And rich it no doubt is, not so much in silver and gold, but all that can purchase these metals. A few miles beyond are the salt mines of Khewra and the coal mines of Dandot, that bring crores of rupees every year to the government treasury as revenue. The Katas Lake is in itself a wonder. It is most picturesquely situated, and one cannot help admiring the good taste of men who first conceived the idea of holding an annual fair here. The population consists mostly of Mussalmans and Hindus, all of very polished speech, refined manners and extremely handsome; and they appear to be conscious of the importance of cleanliness of both mind and body. In a word, it is a man-producing *ilaqa* and the family of which Bhai Mati Das was a scion is a particularly distinguished as a man-producing family.

Not much is known of Mati Das himself except that the Sikh chronicles speak of him as a disciple and companion of Guru Tegh Bahadur. The present heads of the family are unable to give any information of historical value; but the little that the Sikh chronicles say of Bhai Mati Das is more than what people would care to speak of most mortals. He could not have been ignorant of the dangerous mission of the Guru. But like a true Muihal, he chose to face death rather than leave his Guru. The Court of the Kazis, presided over by Aurangzeb himself, condemned him to be sawn into two. He submitted to the torture with unflinching courage and wrested admiration from friends and foes alike.

Equally distinguished was the family of Bhai Dayal Chand. The famous Bhai Mani Singh belonged to this noble house. The Sikh chroniclers attribute to Bhai Dayal Chand a tale that depicts his inborn nobility. It is said that he felt so deeply enraged at Aurangzeb's treatment of the saintly Guru Tegh Bhahadur, that he craved permission to invoke the heavenly powers to burn the whole Turk empire to ashes. How he could have done this, is difficult to say. But of this there can be no doubt that oppression and tyranny carry with them the seeds of destruction, and that empires, no less than individuals, are subject to the same law of

Karma which contains the warning, "Sow the wind, reap the whirlwind." The Guru knew this and pacified his zealous follower by advising him to submit to the will God, which he did, and cheerfully too. The decision in his case was simply diabolic. He was killed by boiling.

No account of the martyrdom of Guru Tegh Bahadur can be complete without a mention being made of a Ranghreta Sikh. Bhais Mati Das and Dayal Chand had, at least, this satisfaction that the Guru was a witness to their sufferings for him. This martyr laid down his life in the effort to save the dead body of the Guru from the possible nay probable, disrespect at the hands of Turks. To secure this, he conceived the idea of substituting his own body for that of the Guru. When he broached the matter to his son the latter insisted that he should be given the honour of martyrdom. Upon this a discussion ensued between the father and the son, and it was not till the father had clinched the argument by pointing out the risk of detection at sight of a young body, that the son at last agreed to cut off his father's head. The headless trunk was then carried to the dungeon where the Guru's trunk lay, the latter being quietly removed to Rakab Ganj for cremation. On this spot now stands a Gurdwara, which is a place of Sikh pilgrimage. The Turks failed to notice the adroitness of the brave act. They took the headless body that they found as that of the Guru, and hacked it into pieces, which were hung on the various gates of Delhi to become the food of crows and vultures. By this unique example of devotion, this martyr won the crown of martyrdom and ennobled the name of his race. He belonged to the lowest order of the untouchable classes in the Punjab. Thenceforward his clan rose at once to power ano affluence. When Guru Govind Rai heard of this uniqne sacrifice, he shouted with joy, "Ranghrete Guru ke bete,"—Ranghretas are Guru's offspring—and Guru's sons they did become. The baptized Sikhs treated them as their own kith and kin. It was only when they forgot the basic principles. of their vitalizing creed and became haughty on coming into possession of pelf and power that the Khalsa[1] again practically lapsed into old ways and practices.

1. Guru Govind Singh was known as Guru Govind Rai before he established the Khalsa Panth. The name Khalsa [pure] in this book, applies to the baptised followers of Guru Govind Singh. The term 'Sikh' denotes men who followed the previous nine Gurus. It also applies to the Khalsa.

CHAPTER IV

PRINCES AJIT SINGH AND JUJHAR SINGH AND BHAI SANT SINGH

The citadel of Anandpur, built not by a ruler with considerable resources at his command and with power to impress labour, could not of course be a pretentious edifice,-and certainly it could not stand a protracted sige on the part of armies sent by Aurangzeb and reinforced by the troops of the Hill Rajas and the hosts of Turk fanatics drawn from all over the Punjab. Still the brave Khalsa garrison withstood the furious attacks of the myriads of assailants for months. Totally cut off from the outer world they, not unoften, made reprisals, in the small hours of the morning, not only to thin the ranks of the unscrupulous foe, but also to provide themselves with such provisions as they could lay their hands on. This state of things, however, could not last long. In an unfortunate moment, the garrison after pourparlers with the enemy vacated the fortress, on the distinct promise, confirmed by oaths on the Koran and the cow, that they should not in any way be molested, and quite against the remonstrances of the Guru that there could be no believing the perfidious Turk and the cowardly Hindu Hill Chieftains. Matters turned out to be exactly as the Guru had predicted. No sooner did the Khalsa contingent leave the precincts of Anandpur, the whole host of the treacher. ous enemy fell upon them. The contest was unequal and it was not long before the Khalsa gave way and despersed in all directions. Some men remained with the Guru who, aided by Prince Ajit Singh, turned back to parry the blows of the enemy till he reached the banks of the Hill torrent, Sirsa. Here the party plunged their horses into the surging flood and escaped to the other bank, whence they proceeded in the direction of Chamkour, where they halted. Night was advancing and the enemy was on the track. In the village, there was a fairly big barn. It was forthwith appropriated and hastily repaired. Meantime the enemy reached the spot in thousands and encamped on the village common, facing the barn. The Guru's followers consisted of only a few dozen intrepid disciples whose sorties, under the cover of darkness, wrought havoc in the ranks of the foe.

In the morning it was decided that there was no use fighting from within the enclosure, and that each and every member of the party should issue forth, engage in a hand-to-hand combat and sell his life as dearly as possible. The lead was taken by Prince Ajit Singh, then only seventeen. With his trusty falchion he boldly fell upon the thickened ranks of the heavily-clad enemy host, and hewed down a large number of them, till he was himself overpowered and received martyrdom. Brave Prince Jujhar Singh only fourteen years old, was standing on the barn-wall along with the Guru, and was witnessing the glorious feats of his valiant martyred brother. The sight of those deeds of heroism inspired his young heart, and he craved permission to take the next place in the ranks of the next day's martyrs. The permission did not take long to come. The Guru helped his darling in putting on his armour and mounting his favourite steed. The brave son of the ever great Guru Govind Singh sailed forth, with the dash and daring of an experienced four-score old commander. The enemy horde was wonder-struck at the sight, and gave way before the boy-warrior's onslaught, and the heads of not a few of them were chopped off as they were receding. The heat of the hard contest and also of the rising sun made the young Prince terribly thirsty. He called out to his father for a draught of water. "Darling," said the Guru, "Ajit (unconquerable) is waiting for thee with a goblet. Go, join him there." This was enough. Thither the cherub-like Jujhar flew and was received in the lap of the Lord of Hosts (1704 A D.)

Night came on and with it came some respite. Of the Guru's followers, only a few survived. They respectfully approached him and requested him to escape into the adjoining country of friendly Malwa Jats, under cover of the night.

which was pitch dark. It was wrong, they argued, to give one's life cheap. If the Guru escaped he would be able to reorganise his forces and punish the hated Turks. There was some wisdom in the suggestion, and so it was accepted. In the party, there was a disciple, Bhai Sant Singh by name, who bore great resemblance to the Guru. . He offered to take the Guru's place and exchange his own uniform with the Guru's The idea was that when in the morning, the enemy came upon him and killed him and his men, they would carry the impression that the Guru and his men had been killed, and so the Guru would not be pursued, at least for some hours. This happened exactly as was hoped it would, and thus did Bhai Sant Singh win the crown of martyrdom, along with Princes Ajit Singh and Jujhar Singh.

CHAPTER V

PRINCES ZORAWAR SINGH AND FATEH SINGH

These two princes were the youngest sons of Guru Govind Singh. Few woman-born have been nobler. They were nearly eight and six years old respectively, when they received martyrdom. When against their solemn oaths, the Hindu Hill Rajas and Aurangzeb's Generals fell upon the Guru and the remnant of his besieged attendents on his evacuation of Anandpur, the latter offered some slight opposition; but they soon gave way before the huge numbers of the foe, and were compelled to disperse. Some were felled down by the swords and spears of the foe, others fled in all directions. The Guru himself, with his two eldest sons, Princes Ajit Singh and Jujhar Singh and a handful of followers, escaped to Chamkor. His wife, Sunder Devi, was safely escorted to Delhi by Apostle Daya Singh, The Guru's venerable mother, mother Gujri, with the two youngest sons of the Guru, Princes Zorawar Singh and Fateh Singh, yielded to the persuasions of their old faimly servant Gangu, a low Brahman, to take shelter in his village, not far off Arriving there, he lost no time in betraying them. This act of treachery brought him some reward from the Mussalman ruler of the place. The old lady and her wards were taken to Sirhind. Bazid Khan, the Governor, held a council of his Ulemas and Kazis, all of whom urged that the boys be either converted to Islam or put to death. The brave sons of the brave father elected the latter alternative. The Nawab of Maler Kotla, who was at that time sitting with Bazid Khan, recommended that the lives of the children be spared; but the Nawab's Hindu Minister, Sucha Nand, to display his zeal for his Mussalman masters, was for the immediate assassination of the children. It was serious mistake, observed this miscreant, to be infatuated with the young ones of a cobra, and nurse them with milk. Even the blood-thirsty Bazid

Khan was struck with horror at the cold-bloodedness of this monster in human form; but the weight of the Ulema's opinion was thrown in favour of Sucha Nand's suggestion. The princes were doomed to be bricked alive in the walls of the Sirhind fortress. The boys heard the sentence without dismay. When they were bricked up to the waist they were called upon by the Nawab to abjure their faith and accept the Kalima of the Prophet. "Begone, miscreant;' replied they,"quench they thirst for blood. We are sons of the great Guru Govind Singh. Fear approacheth us not. We would rather lose our lives at the hands of the *Mulechhas* (the polluted)." This brave retort cost the princes their lives. Immediately, then, their heads were cut off.[1] (1705 A.D.). When the news of this nefarious act was conveyed to the old Mother Gujri, who lay incarcerated in a dungeon close by, she fell down senseless and expired on the spot.

---

1. It is said that the Mohammadan sentries in attendance refused to raise their hands on these innocent children, and that this nefarious deed was done by hired Ghilzai Pathans.

I have visited the scene of this heart-rending tragedy. All the while I was there, a heavy load seemed to weigh me down. I could say nothing and ask nothing, and followed my guide from monument to monument like a walking staute. At length we reached the roof of the dungeon, where the venerable Mother Gujri lay interned and where she expired. I bade my companion to retire. The ground seemed to give way under my feet, and it required no small effort on my part to compose myself and recline against the parapet to the north, just the spot made sacred by the touch of the Mother's feet. That sacred spot I washed with my tears, which flowed in an incessant stream. Where so much water had lain concealed I cannot say; nor can I say how long I should have remained transfixed to the spot, had I not been called to myself by the ekka-driver, who had engaged to take me back to the railway station to catch the train to Ludhiana, where I was then posted as an Inspector of Schools.

Few misdeeds in history have been so swiftly and so adequately punished as those of Bazid

Khan and of the men who shared with him the responsibility of the atrocious decision to take the lives of two innocent children, in such an inhuman fashion. A wave of horror spread over the entire land. Not many years elapsed before a huge army of men, burning with the thirst for revenge, and of dacoits yearning for opportunities for plunder, assembled under the banner of Banda the Brave, and laid siege to Sirhind. Bazid Khan was defeated and slain and thus he received retribution. Sucha Nand was publicly beheaded and he thus met his deserts Any number of Maulvis and Kazis were put to the sword. Mosques were desecrated and burnt. The bodies of Mussalman Pirs and saints were disinterred and cremated-a mode of disposal abhorrent to Moslems. In a word, all sorts of excesses that an infuriated soldiery could conceive of, were committed. Indeed, it seemed as if the denizens of hell had been let loose on earth.

No vestige of old Sirhind now remains except the mausoleum of Shaikh Abdul Qadir, a Mussalman saint, who is said to have come and settled here in the time of Mahmud of Ghazni, and whose saintly life and zeal for the propagation of Mussalman faith have won for him a world-wide renown A visitor devoutly inclined cannot fail to be inspired by the sanctity of the place. The sight of a batch of Mussalman youths, from the remote corners of the earth, dressed in the simplest garments and with faces beaming with purity, peace and contentment, receiving instruction in their holy books with an ardour quite their own, was indeed a spectacle worth seeing. Little did these innocent ones know how

> "Man's inhumanity to man,
> Makes countless thousands weep."

CHAPTER

THE FORTY IMMORTALS

In Sikh history, there are few incidents so pathetic as that pertaining to the treatment meted out to the deserters who left the Guru at Anandpur on signing the "Bedawa,"[1]—during the critical times of its last siege. They became objects of hatred to men, and their women would tolerate them only if they moved about in female garb. Life under such conditions was unbearable. They soon repented, and when they heard that the Mughal forces were running about the deserts of Malwa, in search of the Guru, they betook themselves thither, along with a Sikh herione, named Mother Bhago. One night, forty of these men bivouaced close to a tank, near the village of Khidran, since con-

1. The document which the deserters signed, when driven to despeiation by extreme hunger.

secrated by the name of Mukt Sar, the Tank of Salvation. In the morning when they were washing their clothes, they espied the Mughal forces encamped at a short distance. Forthwith they opened fire on the foe, who returned it, with the result that all the brave penitents fell to a man. The Guru was watching this unequal contest from a sand-hill close by and wondering who this party was that had dared present a bold front to such a vast host of Turk regulars, ably commanded by veteran Generals, he betook himself to the scene of action in the vicinity of the tank. To his great astonishment, he saw that the dead warriors were his own men, who had forsaken him in his dire need. Only one, Mahan Singh, was gasping for breath. He recognised the Guru and, in a few broken words, he told his painful tale, mentioning how they had been wandering in his search to ask for his forgiveness, and be again allowed the privilege of fighting for his cause. Luckily, they had got their heart's desire, and still luckier it was that the Saviour himself had come to condone their fault and receive them into favour again. Needless to say that the prayer was forthwith granted, and an assurance was given that the Forty Warriors had won immortality. The Guru paid his tribute of love by hugging each one to his breast, with bedewed eyes, belauding their gallantry and resigning them to the care of the Timeless One.

The names of the Forty Saved Ones are given below Few names in history are remembered with greater fervour than theirs. There is no Sikh living from whose lips a prayer does not go forth every night, therefore his retiring for rest, invoking the blessings of the Most High in the name of the Forty : and rightly so. A people whose hearts enshrine not love and gratitude, swell not with fervour at the mere mention of their benefactor's names, and to whose mind bravery and chivalry make no appeal, had better not live.

At the spot where these heroes laid down their lives (1705 A. D.) there now exists a town called Muktsar. It is a Tahsil town. The fair held here on every Maghi festival, is attended by thousands of Sikhs from all over the country. The population mostly consists of illiterate Jats. They are awakening to the benefits of education, and have now a High School of their own.

THE FORTY

1. Mahan Singh
2. Mahla Singh
3. Darbara Singh
4. Vir Singh
5. Mansa Singh
6. Parsa Singh
7. Gura Singh
8. Ajaib Singh
9. Sher Singh
10. Narayan Singh
11. Sant Singh
12. Parma Singh
13. Sorja Singh
14. Bachitar Singh
15. Mastan Singh
16. Phula Singh
17. Champa Singh
18. Khan Singh
19. Dip Singh
20. Makhan Singh
21. Ganda Singh
22. Sadhu Singh
23. Jiwan Singh
24. Mula Singh
25. Bhag Singh
26. Kapur Singh
27. Mitha Singh
28. Garu Singh
29. Jassa Singh
30. Chuhr Singh
31. Mani Singh
32. Bhag Singh
33. Mansa Singh
34. Taru Singh

35. Bishan Singh
36. Gurbux Singh
37. Hari Singh
38. Bulka Singh
39. Babeka Singh
40. Ram Singh

CHAPTER VII

GURU GOVIND SINGH

The activities of this greatest of great men, that were ever born, were so many and so varied that it is exceedingly difficult to decide in what particular respect he was pre-eminently great. In the whole domain of history, I have not come across one man of a more inspiring personality. He was at once a leader and follower, a prophet and seer a poet and scholar an intrepid soldier and astute tactician —most heroic in times of danger, most amiable and lovable in the days of peace, most loving and sacrificing, and most selfless in all that he did Hence this brief history would be incomplete if it did not contain a brief memoir of this prince of martyrs, whose example it was that pre-eminently inspired most of the Khalsa to seek the crown of martyrdom.

Guru Govind Singh was born at Patna in the year 1666 A. D. on Poh Sudi 7, 1723 Vikrami. His father was then absent in Assam, where he had gone with Raja Ram Singh to settle an outstanding dispute with a prince of Kamrup. The times of his advent were very hard, and the circumstances in which he was bereft of his saintly father, when a mere lad of nine years, have already been described. Aurangzeb's campaign of forcible conversion to Islam of all Hindus and Sikhs was in full swing. A reign of terror prevailed all over Hindu India. The Punjab was, however, the home of a people whom the new Gospel of Baba Nanak had enthused through and through, and whose conversion was, therefore, camparatively difficult. The huntsman's zeal is proportionate to the dangers of the game. The more difficult to catch it, the more serious the effort he makes. The might of the Mughal had prevailed apparently ; the leaders of the Hindus and Sikhs had been caught and put to an ignominous death in Delhi, and it was thought by the tyrannical rulers that the trouble was over.

But they forgot that "though the mills of God grind slowly, yet He grinds exceedingly small." The crime was bound to react on the oppressors, and to this reaction the work of Guru Govind Singh cotributed not a little.

It is absurd to suppose, as some uniformed writers seem to think, that Guru Govind Singh was actuated by a feeling of revenge in all that he did. Which nine year old child has ever conceived, understood and cherished such a feeling, and launched schemes under its inspiration ? But of this there can be no doubt that when he came of age and read the situation, he lost no time in setting it right He was well versed in all learning, then known, and was gifted poet and writer. These gifts he utilised in translating into Hindi (but in Punjabi characters), with the help of 52 writers of note, all that was noble and inspiring in Sanskrit and Persian literatures, and in infusing his followers with a spirit that led them to resist all wrong, and to regard it an act of merit to give their lives in the chastisement of all evil-doers, regardless of their race or creed, caste or colour. The doctrine did not take long to take a firm root and spread, and it is due to this that the Khalsa, though very small in number, were able not only to hold their own, in their struggle with the religious and political hierarchy of the time, but to completely vanquish them in the long run. With this doctrine as the basic principle, Guru Govind Singh established his church, and named it the Khalsa Panth (the Pure Way). He believed in one pure Divinity, whose agent only he regarded himself to be, and from whom, he claimed, he had borrowed the power to destroy evil, and to establish the reign of Virtue in God's world, which man's selfishness and baseness had turned from a paradise into a regular hell. The membership to this Church was confined only to men who swore at baptism to go through all ordeals for their faith, to make all imaginable sacrifices for the emancipation of their fellow-beings and for their all-round uplift, and to start a regular crusade against all vested interests. This aggressive propaganda at once raised against the

Guru a host of enemies. They stay-at-home and hymn-singing followers of the old Gurus failed to understand him, and mostly shrank from him in terror. The conservative Hindus dreaded the advent of a creed that taught the lowest serf to claim equality with the blue-blooded Rajput, and to relegate to a position of comparative inferiority the time-honoured Brahman and the books he believed in.

Christ came to elevate his people, the Jews; but it was the Jews at whose persistent demand he was crucified. Mohammad was born among the Qureshis. He endeavoured to raise and reform them. But the Quresh would have done with him, had he not fled to Madina, away from the centre of their influence. Nanak was a Khatri; but very few Khatris followed him. Govind Rai, likewise, was a Khatri, but very few Khatris cared for him or followed his standard. The Hindus were then groaning under the oppression of the ruling political and spiritual classes, as few in the world had ever done before. The Guru himself was a Hindu. He shed tears of blood at the sad plight he saw them in, and he strove by all means at his command to rescue them from it. But it was the Hindus, headed by the Hill Rajas, who created all the trouble for him. "He came to his own, and his own knew him not," was as true of Guru Govind Singh as it was true of Christ. He was misrepresented to the Subahs of Lahore, Jullundur, and Sirhind ; but they never took the complaints seriously. They sent expeditions under half-hearted commanders, who felt little enthusiasm for wasting their energies in fighting with a man of God, who, they knew, had no worldly object to serve, and who was a friend of the poor and the oppressed of all nationalities and creeds. Expeditions, led by men so inclined, were bound to fail. But this did not dispirit the Rajputs of the Hills. Failing to enlist the sympathy of the local Governors, they waited in deputation upon Aurangzeb who, though bent down by the weight of years, had not yet profited by his varied experience of men and things, and whose thirst for blood was keen as ever. He forthwith gave orders for the declaration of a Jehad (religious war), against the Guru. The Mussalmans of the Punjab responded with an enthusiasm all their own. The Hindus, too,—those who were not afraid of taking up a lance or handling a knife,—rushed to the field on the side of the Guru. An innumerable host assembled round Anandpur, the Guru's place of abode, and laid siege to it The Khalsa garrison, too small in point of numbers, could not cope with this huge army. They made occasional sorties, under cover of darkness, and made the enemy taste something of their valour. Months passed away in this way. At last, when the besieging hosts began to suffer from the scarcity of provisions, and the prospect of the reduction of the fort appeared to be remote as ever, both the Mussalman and the Hindu commanders sent word to say that they would raise the siege if the Guru vacated the fort and left that part of the country for good. The condition of the besieged was no better, it was but natural that they should jump at the offer. On the solemn assurance, given on the Qoran and the cow that they would be allowed to evacuate the citadel unmolested, the garrison marched out. But no sooner had they done so, the whole of the allied force gave them pursuit and showered arrows and bullets upon them. The result was a regular melee. The Khalsa contingent was forced to flee in all directions. The Guru's literary treasure was washed away in the hill torrent of Sirsa that fell in the way. He was separated from his family. His mother with his two youngest sons, aged eight and six respectively, sought shelter in a village close by, there to be betrayed into the hands of the enemy. What befell them subsequently, has been described in another place. The Guru's wife was taken to Delhi by some trusty followers. The Guru himself with some forty faithful attendants, sought shelter in a dilapidated manor at Chamkour which was soon invested. In the encounters, that ensued, his two eldest sons, Princes Ajit Singh and Jujhar Singh, together with most of the besieged, acquitted themselves as men, and died as martyrs. Only half a dozen people remained in the fortress with the Guru. At night, they prevailed upon him to make his escape, which he reluctantly cid. At dawn, the enemy stormed the manor and massacred the remnant of the brave garrison to a man. The Guru wended his way to 'Machhiwara, some miles off. Here he halted for some days and then made his escape by a queer stratagem. Henceforth he had no permanent abode. At last, he left the inhospitable Punjab and sojourned for a couple of years in the sandy wastes to the south-east, the people of which, all of the Barar clan of jats, acknowledge fealty to him. They offered him their services, which were graciously accepted; but the Turk forces seldom dared to molest him in those far-off dreary wastes, and so no occasion arose for utilising the new auxiliaries. His visit to Khidrana in these parts, is an ever-memorable event. Here the Forty Saved who had forsaken him at Anandpur and had repented afterwards, had engaged the pursuing Mughals and had fallen to a man in retarding the progress of the invading hordes. The spark of life had not yet been extinguished in one of the man. When the Guru approached the dying man, the latter took hold of his feet and asked for pardon for himself and his brave martyred companions whose names are given elsewhere in this book. The pardon was of course readily granted.

From here the Guru proceeded to Dina, a village further off in the same *ilaqa*, whose chiefs, Lakhmir and Samir, offered him their hospitality. Here he panned his famous epistle, the Zafar Nama, in reply to Aurangzeb's invitation to come and see him, assuring him that he would favourably consider any representation which he (the Guru) might have to make relating to his troubles with the Hindu Hill Rajas and his own Muslim commanders. In a highly eloquent and bold language, the Guru tells Aurangzeb that he can place no reliance on the emperor's word, and that he has made a serious mistake in waging a wanton war against him; that his own cause is holy, while the Emperor, is unholy. He adds that the victory, a moral one, is already his, and not of the Emperor's whose memory men will curse for all time, whereas his own example will inspire his followers to continue to offer their lives in the thousands, till tyrants like him are dragged from their thrones and humbled to the ground.

But Aurangzeb's days were numbered. One day while the Guru was engaged in compiling the Granth at Damdama Saheb, news reached him of the Emperor's death. Bhai Nand Lal, an admirer of the Guru and a scholar of great renown, implored him to come and help his master, Prince Muazzam, Aurangzeb's eldest son, who had proclaimed himself Emperor under the title of Bahadur Shah. On the receipt of this message, the Guru proceeded to Delhi. A battle was going on between Muazzam and his brother, Prince Azam, when the Guru arrived with a few armed followers. Choosing a place of vantage, the Guru stationed himself there, and espying Azam on an elephant, he discharged his arrow and shot him dead. In gratitude for his help, Bahadur Shah took the Guru with him to Agra where the coronation took place. A short while after, the Emperor proceeded to the Deccan, accompanied by the Guru, to quell some disturbances there.

In the way, the Guru asked that the men responsible for the murder of his innocent sons and for other criminal proceedings in the Punjab, might be handed over to him. But the Emperor evading compliance, the Guru left him in disgust and proceeded to Nanded, a place in the dominions of the Nizam of Hydrabad, Deccan. Here he met Bairagi Lachman Das, a man of great learning and intrepidity, who becoming furiously enraged on hearing the Guru's tale of wrongs, forthwith undertook to organise a punitive expedition. Under the name of Banda or the Slave of the Guru, he issued a proclamation inviting all brave sons of the Punjab to come and assemble under his banner, with a view to chastise the infamous perpetrators of the foul deeds of which he had heard. The call was heartily responded to. Men assembled in thousands, under that brave man of miraculous power. Within a few weeks, the town of Sirhind was invested and razed to the ground. Samana and Mustafabad were burnt, the bodies of Moslem governors and saints were disinterred and set on fire, and the whole Punjab, from the borders of Delhi to Lahore, was given to pillage and plunder. Bahadur Shah hastened to these parts to restore order, but he was soon compelled to return to his capital leaving things to themselves.

Meanwhile, a conspiracy was formed by some Turks in Nanded, the Guru's place of retirement, to assassinate him, in the mistaken belief that his death would be a fatal blow to the revolution to which the tyrannical rule of the Turks had given birth As the Guru was delivering a discourse to his congregation, a Pathan assassin, without a sign of warning, thrust a daggar into his side and put an end to his earthly work (1708 A. D.).

Nothing would have filled the Guru's heart with greater delight than to die fighting in the thick of a fight But his end was far nobler. He died while he was engaged in teaching and in preaching his catholic creed, the basic principle of which was love for all mankind and a wide tolerance, which gave all men the right to worship God as they chose. The acceptance of this creed by the rulers and the recognition of it by the ruled connoted the negation of all despotism and of dogmatism. It did not, therefore, find favour under the conditions that then prevailed, when men scrupled at nothing, and would fain resort to all means, fair or foul, to remove all obstacles in the way of their worldly advancement. Even to-day, a creed such as this would find little favour with the powers that be. The great Guru Govind Singh, who conceived such a high ideal, some 200 years ago, and laid down his life in its defence, is entitled to the everlasting gratitude of all right-thinking men.

CHAPTER VIII

THE CAREER OF THE HAIDARI FLAG

These were the times of Zakraya Khan, the Turanian Viceroy of Lahore. The blood of the cruel and treacherous Abdul Samad, who had promised quarter to Banda the Brave, but; breaking his word, had him and his associates brutally murdered at Delhi, ran in Zakraya Khan's veins ; and true to his nature, he ruthlessly carried on, to the finish, the campaign for the slaughtering of the Khalsa What his itinerant army did in the central districts of the Punjab, the country called Manjha, will be described, elsewhere, in these pages. This chapter relates to the history of the Haidari Flag. Under this flag assembled the flower of the entire Turk Punjab, with the object of making an herculean endeavour to extirpate the bearded ruffians—the name by which they remembered the Khalsa-who had so impertinently dared to throw down the gauntlet to the heaven-born Turk, who had held undisturbed sway in the Punjab for over five centuries. The tortures to which Banda the Brave and his indomitable companions had been subjected would, it was thought, inspire terror and extinguish the flame that the great Guru Govind Singh had lit. But the time for the realization of that hope did not seem to be approaching. The Sikh problem was becoming more and more knotty.

It is drawing too much on one's imagination to assume that such great questions as the disadvantages of foreign domination swayed men's minds at all. The Turks were no longer foreigners. They were as good Punjabis as the Hindus and the Sikhs. Revenge also had little to do with tension that then existed. True, the incidents that had figured so prominently, during the latter part of the reign of Aurangzeb and during those of Bahadur Shah and Farrukh Syer, and had resulted in the end of Guru Tegh Bahadur, his brave companions, and his illustrious son and grandsons, were still fresh in people's memory. But Bairagi Banda of immortal fame had more than avenged all these acts, and with his end the chapter of blood-feuds ought to have closed. The roots of the discontent lay deeper. It was a war of ideals that was being waged not of great or petty animosities. The Sikhs wanted to live and let others live. But this was not what the Turks wanted. Theirs was a highly organised community, with lofty ambitions. But in those ambitions there was no place for their non-muslim neighbours. Their education and culture and sense of national advancement—all—tended to make them highly aggressive. And every endeavour that brought them what belonged to the non-Moslem neighbouring communities, and every effort that aimed at the weakenig of non-Muslims were looked upon as meritorious deeds. So, when they saw that the Sikhs were not only prepared for resistance; but even for actual retaliation, they began to give serious consideration to the situation.

With this view, in response to an appeal from

influential personages, thousands of Turk notables assembled at Lahore, where it was resolved to supplement the Government endeavour by raising a territorial army, and sweeping off the entire Sikh population from their habitations in the country by one big haul. A deputation of select Pirs, Hajis and Kazis, attended by a host of young fire-brands, waited upon Nawab Zakraya Khan and explained their object to him. This man readily accepted their cordial offer of assistance. So this un-official campaign against the Khalsa was launched under official blessings. On an Id day, the Haidari Flag was hoisted. The cry of 'religion in danger' was raised, and all men of military age, who could weild a weapon, or who wished to share in the spoil of victory, were invited to join the standard. In response to the invitation thousands of mounted men assembled all round Lahore, extending over several miles. The number of men on foot was still more numerous. All classes and tribes were represented. Balochs and Syeds Mughals, and Pathans; Bhattis, Jats, Ranghars and Rajputs—even

Telis,[1] Mochis,[2] Dooms[3] and Julahas,[4] and Gujjars, Dogars, Sainis, and Arains--all--were attracted by promises of reward. Leaders like Taqqi Mohammad and Inayat Khan, raised an army of their own and equipped it at their own expense. Tajar Beg and Murtza Khan came, believing that the slaughter of the Khalsa would be an act of merit both in the eyes of God and man. Babar Beg and Haji Beg joined the conflict to parry swords with the Khalsa and thus, earn distinction. The infamous Yar Mohammad Kazi, and the notorious tell-tale Mullah Pir Mohammad, ran to the spot to weave their nut of intrigue. The great Mughal Sardars of Jullundur, Inayat Ullah, Rajput of Tirawari, and Rohillas from further east, brought their own contingents. Pahar Mal, a great-grandson of Todar Mal of historic fame, lost to all sense of honour and self-respect, placed his vast ill-gotten treasures at the disposal of the leaders of this so-called religious war against the Khalsa.

1. Oil-manufacturers
2. Shoe-makers
3. Low minstrels
4. Weavers

This huge force, supplied with guns and munition by the Nawab, marched out under the command of Mir Inayat Ullah, with the beat of drums and with banners flying. Their hands these men coloured with *mehndi* and they wore festoons on their wrists; as if they were proceeding to win brides for themselves. The thunder of their cannon shook the heavens above, and the heavy trump of their horses and elephants, and of the men on foot, made the earth creak under their weight. The first place of halt was in the vicinity of the Shalamar gardens, where the force, consisting of lacs of men, rested for a considerable time to draw up plans for a concerted action.

The Khalsa, on their part, when apprised of the danger, left their homes, and took shelter in a bush in the middle of the Kahnowan lake. Not much time elapsed before their number reached twenty thousand. The Turk forces, seeing the central districts thus depleted of their fighting men, soon entered to ransack and plunder them. The atrocities they committed on this occasion it is impossible for pen to describe, or for tongue to recount. Suffice it to say that, when the harrowing tale reached the Khalsa, they emerged from their place of shelter and, after an arduous march, they fell upon the huge Turk army, at the dead of night, like enraged lions, and wrought immense havoc. It was a night of midsummer. The enemy had retired late, and their inflated nostrils were roaring like the bellows of a smithy, drowning the tramp of the Khalsa cavalry. They rose in panic and fled in all directions. The Khalsa cut off huge numbers of them as if they were so many sheaves of corn. Large quantities of ammunition and a great number of horses fell into the hands of the Khalsa, with which they speedily ran back to the dense bush, and concealed themselves there. At day-dawn the enemy followed them; but they could not go far enough into the bush. They were mostly heavily clad which rendered their movements difficult. Their flowing coats and loose, bulging trousers were caught in the nettle of the bush like the horns of a stag. The Khalsa, on the other hand, moved about the bush with the litheness of a deer. They had got accustomed to such a life, thanks to the repressive policy of the aggressive tyrants. They lived upon venison, roasted or unroasted, and on the leaves of trees and herbs of the forest, and enjoyed such meals exceedingly. The enemy, tired of fruitless persuit, set fire to the bush. When the Khalsa had to come out, perforce, and face their assailants with the ferocity of lions. The cries of anguish and Allah ! Allah ! rent the sky. The Khalsa fought with desperate bravery. The blows of their weapons fell upon the enemy like hammers, and crushed them under their weight. This did not discourage the enemy, however. Not a few of them fought with valour, and gladly laid down their lives, in the sure belief that they would rise from their graves to have 'Houries' in their embraces. The struggle was, however, unequal. Only six or seven thousand Khalsa were opposed to lacs of Turks. When has an infinitely small force destroyed a huge army unless, of course, the Divine hand was at the back of the former ? As the brave Arjuna and his four brothers vanquished innumerable hosts under the great veterans Bhishama, Dronacharya and Karuna, in the great war of Mahabharata, as Sugriva and Hanuwant, Angad and Jamawant, the devoted followers of Sri Ramchandra, broke down the power of the mighty Ravana, the great Sea-Lord, similarly, the Khalsa, aided by the Divine Being Himself, inflicted a heavy loss on the enemy, scattering them in all directions, before they themselves returned to their hiding place.

About sixty thousand Turks still remained behind, and gave chase to the Khalsa who, however, were difficult to get at. They were scattered all over the country. Some hovered round Lahore, some round Sialkot, some in the country, and others round Amritsar. They concealed themselves during the day; and when night came, they fell upon the enemy, obtained good deal of booty, and then returned to their abodes in the forest unmolested. One of these parties, consisting of two thousand brave men, was roaming about the Ravi when a heavy downpour of rain came on. Close by was the village of Bharatpur. They made towards it and took shelter in the house of a Kshatrya, Bhagwant by name. He received them kindly and did his best to entertain them. It was months since the Khalsa had the luck to taste human food, and they were offering thanksgiving for being so favoured, when, lo ! the enemy, getting scent of their arrival, came and invested the house. For a considerable time, the Khalsa gallantly defended themselves, and kept back the enemy; but this they could not do for long. At last the door of the hospitable Kshatrya's house was broken open, and the enemy rushed in. Immediately, then, in response to the prayers of the Khalsa, the Lord came to their help, as he had done to protect Prahlad from his cruel father, and as He had saved the honour of Droupodi of sacred memory. Rain poured in torrents and the tents and the equippage of the Turks were swept off by the tempest. The Khalsa then came out of their sheltering place and reached the forest.

The sky again cleared and the Turk army had a much-needed respite They buried their dead and, cutting off the heads of the Khalsa.

who had fallen in the battle, near the village of Bharatpore, they carried them off as trophies to Lahore, with drums beating and banners flying, believing that they had annihilated the Khalsa completely and that the handful, who had fled, as they thought, would never dare show their face again anywhere in the Punjab. A messenger ran post-haste to the Nawab to convey to him the glad tidings. The Nawab congratulated himself on his good luck The Prophet, he thought, had really come to his help. He was actually picturing to himself the prospect of seeing the whole Punjab converted to Islám. He sent word to the commander to halt with his victorious army at the village of Bhilowal, in the neighbourhood of Lahore from where he would himself escort it to the capital with due splendour and pomp. But this was not to be. The Khalsa, who had escaped from Bharatpure, and joined the other Jathas* who, as said above, were hovering about Lahore. Their wrath knew no bounds, when they heard of the treat accorded to their

*Parties

dead. Immediately they resolved to inflict a severe chastisement on the Turks who were making themselves merry at Bhilowal. This was no sooner said than done. Scouts brought the news that the Turks were enjoying deep slumber. The Khalsa, then, prostrated themselves before the Almighty for strength to put down the Turk rule which was responsible for the slaughter of their dear ones and of the cow, an animal who was as mother to them all, to which they owed so much of glory and prosperity, and whose extinction was tantamount to their own extinction. The Ravi was crossed at midnight, when the Khalsa advanced, sedate and calm, sternly resolved on teaching the enemy a lesson which they should long remember. And so the Akal Purkh had ordained that it should be. The enemy were taken unawares. They had spent the night in drink and debauch, and there were not a few who were engaged in holding the rehearsal of dances and music with which it had been resolved to march in state to Lahore. Some lay dead asleep like logs of wood; others had gone out early in search of *shikar*. Others, again, were engaged in their religious exercises, and were disturbing the quiet haunts of wolves and hyenas in the jungle round Bhilowal. Upon this scattered and disorderly mob fell eight thousand Khalsa with the suddenness of lightning. Down went their 'safajangs', and their bullets worked with such precision that whole ranks of Turks fell in regular array, as if they were having a drill parade They fled in terror, leaving their valuables and weapons behind. When munition was all spent, the Khalsa drew out their *kirpans* and slew huge numbers of the flying enemy. The cowardly Maulvis, Mullahs and Kazis allowed themselves to be cut down like sheep, without striking one blow for their faith, or for their own life or honour. The great Turk leaders, who had brought their contingents in the aid of the Lahore Subah, all fell in the action. Mullah Mir Mohammad, the principal organiser of this Jehad against the Khalsa, and his numerous following, fell to rise no more. Some Turks were cut down while fleeing; some struck against the trees and other impediments and fell, some broke their limbs; some lost their eyes. There was, in fact, no one, who had not lost his near or dear ones in this unforunate war. The houses of most Mussalmans in the Punjab and also in Rohil-Khand, which had also sent its contingent, were houses of mourning. This was how the Lord smote the enemy and poor Zakraya turned in his bed. In rage the standard-bearer tore down the Haidari Flag and set it on fire. This happened in 1721 A.D.

CHAPTER IX

BHAI TARA SINGH

The charge against this brave man was that he had harboured the Khalsa at his house in the village of Dhilwan in Manjha. He had incurred the anmity of Sahib Rai, Lambardar of the village of Nowshera. This minion, dressed in brief authority, rope roughshod over the feelings of poor villagers. His horses used to be let loose to graze on the fields of the peasantry; but no one dared to drive them out. Those of the peasants, who professed the faith of the Khalsa, were the objects of his special hatred; simply because they were in official disfavour, and hence easy to fleece. To the poor peasantry, who depended only on the produce of their lands, and had no other occupation or profession to eke out a living, this unchecked browsing of the animals on their fields meant starvation and death. The Khalsa, who suffered the most, driven to desperation, went to the Lambardar and complained to him. This pretty Revenue Official became furious, and charged them with ingratitude. They were, said he, regular dacoits and felons, members of a gang whom it was criminal to harbour in his village. Instead of being thankful for receiving the wherewithals of subsistence and shelter, they had the hardihood to come and accuse him of trespass and theft: for that was what their complaint ammounted to. He would report them to the authorities and make them feel what the insult to him meant. The poor Khalsa peasants, seeing that they could expect no redress of their wrongs, left the village for good. Continued stay their only meant hunger and starvation. Bhai Tara Singh, who was highly religious man, endowed with a generous heart hearing of their sad tale, sent for them and undertook to give them board and lodging until they could shift for themselves.

Now, it so happened that a few days after the aforesaid peasants had left Nowshera, the mares of Sahib Rai were stolen in broad day-light, while they were grazing unchecked as before. His suspicion fell on these poor peasants. Bhai Tara Singh was asked to deliver them into his custody, so that they might be taken to the Kazi and punished for the alleged crime. But the Bhai, believing them to be innocent, as indeed they were, refused to surrender them. Thereupon the Lambardar proceeded to Patti and lodged a formal complaint with the city Magistrate, Mirza Ja'far Beg, against Bhai Tara Singh who, he said, was an old rebel, whose house was the rendezvous of innumerable bad characters. They committed raids all over the land, and the lives and the property of the people were insecure. If an example was not made of the man, and the other peasantry began to imitate him, the whole population would be in ferment. The best course, therefore, was to nip the insurrection in the bud; for though the cloud was, then, no bigger than a man's hand, it might spread and overcast the whole sky, darkening the entire political horizon. The Magistrate listened to the tale with rapt attention; and expressed great astonishment that the villages under his jurisdiction should be so insecure. He took the mendacious statemens of the Lambardar as a gospel truth, and marched against the small Khalsa colony with a detachment of a few hundred cavalry under the command of a nephew of his. It was intended to take the place by assult, at the dead of night, and so would it have been, had not Baghel Singh, a valiant soldier, who was an early riser, been out at the time to perform his ablutions. With a brass pot full of water, in one hand, and a small axe in the other, he was proceeding in the direction of a jungle when he saw, emerging from the thicket, a host of Turk soldiers advancing in military array. The brave man at once blocked their way, so that the Khalsa might not be taken by surprise. He challenged the advancing host to fight their way out, and then fell upon them as a tiger would do on a herd of sheep, and with one stroke cut the head of a nephew of the commander in two. Another nephew also met the same fate, when, roused to fury, the commander himself darted on Baghel Singh and pierced him through with his spear. The brave Baghel Singh fell; but the Khalsa colony was saved. The noise and tumult of the fray had roused them all. They marched out fully armed; but before they could give battle, the enemy had retreated under the orders of the commander, whom the loss of his two nephews had completely disspirited.

The struggle now took another form. The ruler of Patti lost no time in approaching the Governor, Khan Bahadur Zakraya Khan, and succeeded in persuading him to send a punitive expedition, consisting of 4,000 men, under the command of General Moman Khan, a cruel, relentless person of dare-devil spirit, who scrupled at nothing. .The report of the preparations of the expedition spread like wild fire. Daily in the open space, outside the Lahore fort, innocent men, women and children of the Khalsa faith were publicly racked, pilloried and gibbeted. In the same open space, there was a well, which was provided with wheels at every turn of which the limbs of the

Khalsa, bound to them, were broken asunder and crushed. This was done presumably to strike the populace with awe. Little wonder, then, that men should have approached Bhai Tara Singh, with the request to offer submission or to fly into jungles and take shelter there, The Bhai listened to them patiently , but he refused to consider the proposal to come to terms with the Turks. Submission to Turk authority, said he, would mean the abandonment of the programme chalked out for the Khalsa. The Khalsa were there to oppose all evil. He believed that Turk rule was a curse on Indian humanity. The king, according to the traditions of all oriental nations, was the shadow of God. If he was not inspired by high ideals, if his representatives all over the land were low, lustful libertiness, who had one law for their own kith and kin and another for all non-Muslims, who considered it an act of merit to rob, plunder and forcibly convert all non-Mussalmans to their faith, and who put to death all dissenters, the only course left to all honest men was to raise the standard of revolt and die in the struggle. He knew he was a poor cultivator, without considerable following, and that it was certain death for him to oppose the Imperial forces; but he was sorry he could take no other course. If there were men who thought safety was better, and who believed it was good to retire to the jungles, and wait for a better opportunity to fall upon the foe, they were quite free to do so. But he, on his part would, like the moth, fly into the flame, and burn himself there, to rise again, like the phoenix into life eternal.

So, their course was decided upon. The brave Sikh colonists, numbering not more than four hundred souls, marched out from their places of shelter to check the advance of the invading host. The invaders were thousands in number, well equipped, and well provisioned. But this circumstance did not dispirit the Khalsa, whose weapons were mostly crude and resources poor. But their hearts were sound. They knew they were laying down their lives for a sacred cause. This lent them strength to offer resistance' to a formidable foe and to perform acts of prowess that won them unstinted admiration even from their enemies. They were resolved to give their lives, but they took care that the enemy paid for them dearly. Their arrows and quoits, their broad swords and halberds, wrought havoc in the ranks of the enemy. The braggart Taqqi Beg, who had boasted that he would drag Tara Singh alive to Lahore, returned to his camp sans front teeth. Many a Mughal and Turk bravado had their head lopped off and strewn on the ground. One by one, the brave comrades of Bhai Tara Singh fell, after performing wondrous feats of valour. At length, when Bhai Tara Singh was left alone, he sprang into the ranks of the enemy, roaring like a lion, and cleaved his passage with his broad-sword right up to the spot where stood the Mussalman Commander, ridng on an elephant. He aimed a heavy blow at the man; but as he leaped up to reach his antagonist he was surrounded by the latter's lieutenants and felled to the ground. Thus died gloriously in the year 1782 Vik., 1725 A.D. in the month of Phagan the valiant Bhai Tara

Singh who,like Arthur's Knights of the Round Table, had done many a brave deed to free his country from the yoke of the Yavans, giving proof of the invincible spirit that the Khalsa then possessed. On the spot near the village of Khadim Garhi, where his remains were cremated, now stands a temple, where the people of the surrounding villages, who still cherish his memory, assemble every year to do him honor.

CHAPTER X

BHAI MANI SINGH

This great divine of the Khalsa was born at the village of Kobewal, in the Malwa He was a Jat by birth. At the age of seven, when his parents were at Anandpur, on a visit to Guru Tegh Bahadur, he felt such a fond attachment for Govind Rai, the Guru's son, who was of his own age, that he would not part company with him. At the request of the Guru, his parents left him in the custody of Mother Gujri. From that time forward he remained with Govind Rai, the future Tenth Guru, through thick and thin, and with him he shared his board and lodgings The teachers, who taught Govind Rai also taught Mani, Jewel, as he was then called. Thus all the learning, which was possible to acquire, in that age, was equally shared by both. Possessed of a sharp intellect, and discerning mind, Mani soon rose to distinction. Mother Gujri looked upon him as her own child. To the congregation, he was the High Priest. He daily preached the word of God to them and ministered to their comfort. He lent his whole-hearted support to the Tenth Guru in the establishment of the Khalsa Panth, and in all the schemes that the Guru launched forth for raising his people. When the treacherous Mughal commanders, helped by the perfidious Hindu Hill Rajas fell upon the Guru's household on the evacuation of Anandpur, Bhai Mani Singh helped the Guru's wives, Mothers Sundar Devi and Sahib Devi, to disguise themselves in male attire, and escorted them to Delhi through tremendous difficulties. He next accompanied them to Damdama Sahib; where the Guru communicated to them the heart-rending intelligence of the bricking-up alive of Prince Zorawar Singh and Fateh Singh in the walls of Sirhind by the Turk Governor of the place. Bhai Mani Singh then accompanied the Guru to the Deccan, and when the Guru saw that his end was approaching, he sent him back to Delhi to attend upon his wives and to look after their interests. These duties he performed with rare devotion and fidelity When a dispute arose between the followers of Baba Banda and the Tatya Khalsa regarding the distribution of the offerings at the Golden Temple at Amritsar, Mother Sundar Devi deputed him to visit the place and bring about a sattlement. The local Khalsa accorded him a hearty reception, and prayed to him to take charge of the temple himself. He accepted their prayer and set himself to the task of correcting the abuses, that had crept into the mode of Khalsa worship. The days of his pastorate were the best in the Khalsa annals. His learning and high scholarship, his masterly exposition of the Scriptures, and his saintly life and genial disposition, commanded unstinted admiration and drew immense congregations. It was in these days that he conceived the idea of revising the Ad Grath, with a view to sort out the hymns of each of the Gurus and Bhagats, scattered all over the Book, and divide from one another the words of the text of which it was composed, and punctuate the various phrases and sentences. This highly commendable step had to be abandoned owing, partly, to the ignorant opposition that was raised; but principally, to the protracted anguish, caused by the incessant slaughter of innocent co-religionists, before his very eyes, a fate which he was himself destined to share, not long after.

The Turks in those days did not confine themselves to the molestation of Khalsa men and women, and to the burning and plundering of their houses In their fury, they did not spare even places of Sikh worship. They took pleasure in defiling and desecrating them and razing them to the ground. Some of the more important were converted into mosques, or places of business, or were kept locked up. The Golden Temple at Amritsar shared the general fate. Sentinels were placed at its entrance and no one was allowed admission During these days of travail, the influence of Bhai Mani Singh stood the Sikhs in good stead. His Mussalman friends approached the authorities and had the orders for closing the Temple to public worship rescinded. The Bhai was thus enabled to resume his work ; but the congregations were too small for the work to be carried on. For fear of the Turks, people dared not leave their homes in large numbers, even to attend worship. It occurred to the Bhai that, perhaps, gold might mollify the Turks and secure for the Khalsa the resumption of worship at the Amritsar Golden Temple. He formally submitted his proposal to the local magistrate, Abdur Razak. who held out hopes of a favourable consideration by the Subah of Lahore, Zakriah Khan. The latter accepted the proposal on condition that Rs. 10,000 be paid to the Government. The sum demanded was apparently an exorbitant cne ; but the Bhai hoped against hoped to be able to raise the amount from the offerings made by the worshippers. Notices were issued for the holding of a fair at the Temple. The annoncement was received with joy. Even in distant places people began to make preparations for attending the fair. Days before the appointed date, multitudes poured into the city of Amritsar and the hope was entertained that the income would be large enough to allow the payments of the promised contribution. But it was not to be. The Devil put into the head of Zakriah Khan, commonly called Khan Bahadur, to take worshippers by surprise on the day of the fair, and put them to the sword. With that view, he sent a detachment of Infantry and Cavalry, with orders not to allow a single Khalsa to escape. But somehow, before his men reached Amritsar, his intentions became known. The result was the immediate dispersion of the visitors. In a few hours, not a single Khalsa could be seen in Amritsar. This discomfiture enraged the blood-thirsty Khan Bahadur. He sent for Bhai Mani Singh and took him to task for the conspiracy to defraud the Government. The Bhai was, of course, not at all to blame. It was the miscreant Khan Bahadur who was in fault. But when were despots ever conscious of their own shortcomings? Forthwith he ordered that the Bhai be placed under arrest, and brought to him on some convenient day. When the Bhai was produced before him, he again demanded the payment of the contract money. The Bhai said that he was a poor priest, that the promise had been made on the understanding that there would be offerings; but that the scheme having proved abortive, he was unable to find the requisite money. Seeing that he could extort nothing from the Bhai, Khan Bahadur told him that he would let him off on dondition that he accepted Islam and employed his learning in preaching a religion which, he thought, was far superior to the one which the Bhai professed, and which inclucated the worship of One True God and the brotherhood of man. In forensic ability, the Bhai was matchless. He questioned the truth of the Subah's allegations and emphatically declared that for no consideration would he swerve from his loyalty to the Guru. The Bhai's case was referred to the Maulvis, interpreters of religious law. They pronounced against the Bhai and ordered his limbs to be torn off This was publicly done (1738 A.D.) and the Bhai's remains were cremated at the spot near the Fort called the Shahid Ganj*-the scene

*"In this enclosure (Shâhid Ganj) are also the

of many an act of barbarity like this. The news of the cruel deed infuriated the Khalsa throughout the land. They retaliated by committing raids from their abode in the wild forests and barren wastes. Many a tyrant had to suffer for his crimes, and many profligates who had forcibly removed Hindu and Khalsa girls into their seraglios, were stabbed in their beds. Government outposts were attacked and the treasures were looted : this being the only way that then lay open to get back at least a part of the property that had been confiscated under the arbitrary orders of the cruel rulers of those days.

samadhs (tombs) of Bhai Mani Singh and Gulzar Singh both faithful followers of Guru Govind Singh and constant attendants on him. Bhai Mani Singh was a poet of the Punjabi language and he composed the Granth of Guru Govind Singh a beautiful verse They were both residents of Anandpur Makhowal, where the Guru usually lived, and had come on a visit to the Darbar Sahib at Amritsar, when they were seized by the king's officers and brought to Lahore, where they were publicly executed on the 5th of Saffar 1140 A.H. (1127 A D.) during the viceroyalty of Mir Manu (Zakriya Khan).—S. Mohd. Latif's Lahore, p. 162.

CHAPTER XI

BHAI BOTA SINGH

It is a mistaken notion that attributes the birth of military spirit in the Khalsa to the Tenth Guru. Khalsa militarism, in fact, dates from the time when, the Turk rulers took it into their heads to persecute the Sikhs. Even a mouse would, when brought to bay, turn round and face his enemy. After the days of Banda the brave, it became an article of creed with Mussalman potentates not to give quarter to the Khalsa. Successive conferences were held at the residence of the Subah of Lahore, which were attended by fief-holders and Jagirdars, both Hindu and Mussalman, who owed their importance to Government patronage, at which the Subah appealed for popular support in eradicating the influence of the Khalsa. He held out hopes of reward to all who would help in the undertaking. Rapacious harpies and lickspittles, who always congregate round the powers that be, are ever on the look-out for such opportunities. Such were the heartless, soulless and ghoulish creatures that formed the audience of the Subah. They acclaimed the Subah's speech; and assured him that they were all ready to lay their lives, their hearths and homes, at the feet of the Government was to joyfully carry out orders issued to them. At one of these conferences it was publicly given out that the policy of the Government was to destroy the Khalsa, root and branch. To effect this, it was thought necessary to put to death all Sikhs without regard to sex or age. Their property was to be forfeited to the State. Their houses were to be burnt, and they were to be hunted down like wild beasts in their far-off haunts and retreats. The official heirarchy eagerly gave effect to the orders, and the un-official Hindu and Mussalman notables vied with one another in this vicious compaign. The result might well be imagined. Every village, every hamlet, every town served as a slaughter house, where God's innocent creatures were butchered, Every tree served as a gibbet and every dark, neglected well became a Drug* into which people, professing the Khalsa faith, or men, suspected of being in sympathy with them were thrown indiscriminately, and were then left to die of hunger, or be stifled by their foul and poisonous stench. In a surprisingly brief period, the whole land was cleared of the Khalsa. Their houses were pillaged plundered or set on fire, and men, women and children were mercilessly bayoneted. Some of them fled to the far-off jungles and there sought the protection, which their own fellow-beings denied them. Not a few hid themselves in caverns, away from the haunts of men, to be subsequently captured and put to a horrible end. Not unoften these haunts were discovered by search parties, who never failed to pile up logs of wood at their entrances and set fire to them The inmates were smoked up like a veritable nest of hornets, and no one ever hear the tale of their sufferings.

---

* A dark well whereinto criminals were thrown to die.

Phai Bhota Singh was one of these men. Like Bhai Tara Singh, he was a Manjha Sikh. He wandered about in wastes and jungles and lived upon the bark and leaves of trees. Sometimes, under cover of darkness, he would visit human habitations in search of food. But this he generally failed to get, for he would not let anyone see him, for fear of being arrested. On one occasion, a party of zamindars met him by chance, and were surprised to see that Khalsa should have been allowed to wander about freely in that manner. One of the party suggested that the strange figure might be a "Bahurupia" one of the troupe of itinerant professional actors, who went about the country masquerading, and who lived on doles of food given in lieu of the performances they gave. How could a brave Khalsa, they argued, play the game of hide-and-seek, when his co-religionists were being tortured to death? Bhai Bota Singh heard the remarks and was cut to the quick. To be charged with leading the life a coward by an uncouth rustic ! The very thought was harrowing. Forthwith he resolved to make himself know and suffer martyrdom. Close by was an inn, built by one Nur-ud-din, near Tarn Taran. It lay neglected and was in a dilapidated condition. Bhai Bota Singh stationed himself there. With the help of another comrade, he effected the necessary repairs and made it secure against sudden attack. During the day, the two men served the way-fares and supplied them their meals, as did inn-keepers in those times. They kept themselves informed of what was going on in the country. They knew who tyrannized over the people. Hindu parents complained to them that their boys and girls had been snatched from them by this magnate or that Nawab. When night fell, they would arm themselves with clubs and hatchets, break open the door of the miscreants, give them a short shrift and restore the kidnapped children to their parents. Whatever they could lay their hands upon they carried off as booty and distributed it among the poor and the needy. Thus they avenged many a wrong, and rescued many an innocent maiden from a life of infamy. But this could not remain secret for long. The Subah of Lahore and the Delhi Emperor had just exchanged congratulations on the total annihilation of the Khalsa, and the consequent peace in the land. The news of the devastation caused by these two intrepid Khalsas and the helplessness of the people of their own faith, alarmed and distressed them. They had not yet, however, reached the end of their tether. To kill two men, a regular regiment was despatched with necessary accoutrements and supplies. The inn was besieged. Many were the men whom the missiles of Bhai Bota Singh and his companion from behind the parapet, pierced through and through. Some were killed, and a great many were wounded. At last the place was taken by assault, and both the valiant Khalsas received martyrdom, fighting heroically with their foes (1739 A.D.) The Mughal regiment, greatly reduced, returned to the capital, beating drums of victory. The fact, however, could not be concealed that only two men had necessitated such large military operations. The way in which the two martyrs had fought and met death, elicited admiration, and the conviction grew upon the minds of the populace that the transfer of the Government to the hands of the Khalsa could not be long delayed

CHAPTER XII

SARDARS MAHTAB SINGH AND SUKHA SINGH

While the events, recorded in the last three chapters were happening, while fire and sword were devastating the land, such of the Khalsa as loved peace left their hearths and homes to take shelter in distant lands, where Turk influence was not so predominant. Of these refugees was Sardar Mahtab Singh of Miran Kot, a village in the vicinity of Amritsar. He had taken up service in Bikanir, one of the principal states of Rajputana. But the love of home still blazed in his breast, and his ear was always bent upon news from his native land. The service of the Khalsa and of the places of Sikh worship was to him a passion. At his new home in Bikanir, visitors from the Punjab were always sure of a cordial welcome. One of his guests once brought him a piece of news that simply stunned him. The Golden Temple at Amritsar had been taken possession of by one Massah, a Mussalman Ranghar, and was being daily defiled. In the Hari Mandir (Holy of Holies), the miscreant daily held *nautches* (dances). Broken bottles of wine lay scattered about in the enclosure. Wine flowed into the Tank of Immortality and polluted it. Lewd and depraved young men and women loitered about, for hours, where the scriptures were previously recited and hymns sung in praise of the Lord. The blood-curdling details sent a thrill of horror into the frames of the hearers. Forthwith Sardar Mahtab Singh resolved to visit Amritsar, and make an example of the miscreant Massah. He ordered his steed to be brought to him and rode at a gallop, taking with him Sardar Sukha Singh of Kambho Mari. The way led through arid wastes, scantily populated, and inhabited by people mostly inhospitable. At places, they had actually to fight their way forward. Arriving at Amirtsar, they bathed in the sacred tank and then went to the bazar, where they purchased a few bags.

filled them with some coins and, dressed as revenue collectors, they presented themselves at the entrance to the Temple, and peremptorily demanded admission. The sentinels on being informed that the men were officials and had brought money for their master, allowed them to pass on. The entrance into Massah's presence was still easier. No one is more needy and greedy than a confirmed debauchee. The man in waiting escorted the Sardars to the Ranghar's presence with great civility, and offered them seats. These the new-comer would not accept. First they made their obeisance and, when Massah bent down to receive the money, down came Mahtab Singh's falchion from its sheath, like the flash of lightning, and Massah' head rolled on the ground. The dancing girl fell into a swoon, and the companions in debauch of the accursed libertine ran out terror-stricken. Their work done, the brave Mahtab Singh and his companion rode back through the bazars, brandishing their weapons. The hearts of the Turks quailed at the news. A gloom fell over the Turk Punjab, and even the inveterate foes of the Khalsa could not help acknowledging their temerity.

The whole machinery of the Government was set in motion to get hold of the authors found. At length, when Sardar Mahtab Singh happened to pay a visit to his village to see his son, a resident of Jandiala informed the authorities of the fact and had him arrested. His boy was snatched from his arms, and was cruelly flung to the ground, to become the food of kites and vultures. The Sardar himself was taken to Lahore, subject to unspeakable tortures on the wheel and crushed to death (1740 A. D) His head was exhibited in Hira Mandi, and his body was thrown into a ditch.

Sardar Sukha Singh did not survive his brave companion very long. The informers had him arrested and he was cruelly put to death. According to the Sikh chroniclers Sukha Singh was a carpenter by caste. He was loved and respected by the whole Panth for many lovable traits of character. Like King Arthur's Knights, whenever there was a danger to face or some distinguished act of bravery to be done, Sukha Singh's name was the first that suggested itself to every one. He was believed to be a deeply religious man. When a boy, he came under Sikh influence and got himself formally baptised into the Khalsa faith. Lives of men with long hair were, in those days, in great jeopardy. The parents of Sukha Singh became alarmed. They dissuaded him from having anything to do with the Khalsa faith; but they failed to make any impression on him. One night, when he lay asleep, they quietly cut off his hair. When he awoke and saw the outrage done him, and divined the motive, he jumped into a well, close by, to put an end to his life. The noise of the fall attracted some passere by, who ran to his rescue, and forcibly brought him out, rebuking him for the attempted suicide. But Sukha Singh was obdurate, until his parents allowed him to leave their house and take up the service of the Panth. Sukha Singh was thus consecrated to the service of the Guru from his very boyhood, and was destined to play a very important part in Sikh history.

CHAPTER XIII

HAQIQAT RAI THE VIRTUOUS

Haqiqat Rai was born in 1724 A.D. He was the only son of well-to-do Khatri parents of Sialkot. They were both pious Nanak Panthis. Haqiqat had been married for some years to a well-read, cultured Sikh girl, daughter of Sardar Kishan Singh of Batala, in the Gurdaspur district. Both these causes combined to instil deep spirituality into the mind of the young Haqiqat, and although he had not yet formally received baptism as a Khalsa, it was admitted, on all hands, that in religious zeal and devoutness, and in jealous regard for the honour of his creed and country, he was second to none of the professed baptised Sikhs of his time. This is way he came to have the surname 'Virtuous,' though yet a stripling. One day he fell out with his Mussalman teacher, who made disrespectful reference to some Hindu gods. Haqiqat became furious and retaliated by casting similar aspersions on the character of the Prophet of Islam. This was enough to seal the lad's doom. He was forthwith snatched from the custody of his guardian and placed under arrest. By ingenious devices, exaggerated reports of the boy's rude reference to the holy Prophet were spread broad-cast. Men's worst passions were aroused, and Haqiqat's life was threatened even in his own native city where his father, Diwan Bagh Mal, was an official in the local kutchery. But he had friends, even among the Mussalman population, whose humane feelings were roused by his innocent looks and young years. The local authorities, therefore, thought it prudent to take him to Lahore, and hand him over to the Chief Kazi there. The police escort, fearing civil commotion, took him off as quietly as possible. In the small hours of night, as the boy was carried through the avenues, in which he had, erstwhile, played with the fawn of the deer, and sung with the thrush and the nightingale, a wail went forth from the lacerated hearts of the distressed Bhai Bagh Mal and of the boy's mother, Gauran, whom nothing could deter from following their darling boy, and was reverberated through the jungle, startling the wolf and the tiger, as they emerged from their hunts to prowl about in search of food. The sky became cloudy and it began to drizzle, as if the angels, from on high, contributed their quota of tears at the heart-rending sight. In the way, the party halted at Eminabad. Diwan Jaspat Rai, Financial Secretary to Subah of Lahore, who was a resident of the place and, then, happened to be at home, was aproached with request to use his influence on behalf of the boy ; but he turned a deaf ear to the entreaty. His brother, Diwan Lakhpat Rai, was next waited upon at Lahore ; but he appeared to be much more incensed than even Mussalmans themselves The Gevernor was, then, approached by an influential deputation, headed by Diwan Surat Singh, Lala Dargahi Mal and Jamadar Qasur Beg ; but he, too, was hard as adamant. In a word all efforts to save the lad failed. The cruel, blood-thirsty tyrants wanted blood and nothing but blood, and blood they had. After a mouck trial, the order of death was pronounced. The boy received the order calmly, and bowing to his parents he entreated them and the huge crowd of mourners, that had gathered there, not to weep over his loss, for he was not really dying to the soul ; he was only going to live the life eternal. The saintly and heroic lad, whose face shed the serene glory of the Moon, and whose look sent a thrill of joy into many a hears, was chained to a pillar, and caned till he bled and lost all consciousness. He was finally entrusted to the executioner to die on the scaffold (1742). His body taken to a secluded spot near the mausoleum of Shah Balawal, and was there cremated. Whole Lahore turned out to accompany the bier, and ten times as many people joined the procession from the neighbouring villages. A *Samadh* (tomb) stands over the site, and a fair which is very largely attended is held on the premises annually on the Basant Panchmi, about the middle of February. Maharaja Ranjit Singh greatly patronized the shrine and held many Durbars in its inspiring precincts.

Sayed Mohammad Latif thus speaks of this martyr :—Haqiqat, a Hindu boy of 17, used to study in a school. He quarrelled with the mussalman boys and returned the abusive language which they had applied to some of the Hindu gods. He was taken to the Kazi who sentenced him to be executed for daring to abuse the Prophet. The case came before the Governor, who confirmed the Kazi's sentence, declaring, however, that should the boy embrace Islam the sentence might be commuted or set aside altogether. Haqiqat Rai, true to the faith of his ancestors, rejected the invitation to embrace the faith of the Prophet and was executed." ('Lahore', p. 245.)

Haqiqat Rai's father-in-law, Sardar Kishan Singh Upal and his brothers Mal Singh and Dal Singh, later, approached the Khalsa with a request for help in wreaking vengeance on the culprits who were responsible for the cruel murder. The help was readily given. As referred to briefly in a subsequent chapter, the miscreants, who had shown no mercy to the boy martyr, received none when their turn came to ask for it. After a march of 50 miles in one night, the Khalsa made a surprise attack on Sialkot town. Dal Singh slew the Kazi who had condemned Haqiqat to die. The head of the Mullah, who had first provoked Haqiqat Rai and of the Governor, Amir Beg, were exhibited in the market-place. What consolation such a revenge brought to the kinsmen of the martyr and their sympathisers, it is difficult to say; but in this there is no doubt that the savage ruling classes soon came to know that some manliness was still left in the subject people, and that they could not exasperate them with impunity.

CHAPTER XIV

BHAI TARU SINGH

Five minute's walk to the south-west of the Lahore railway station; lies a spot sacred to the memory of the famous martyr, Bhai Taru Singh. It bears the honoured name of Shahid Ganj, the Abode of Martyrs. This distinction it shares with another spot close to the Fort. For over a century, from the days of the martyrdom of Banda the Brave, down to the times when the Sikh Confederacies wrested the supermacy of the Punjab from the Mughals, Turks and Pathans, both these places were the scenes of the martyrdom of thousands of Sikhs who were put to death with unspeakable tortures such as hellish vindicativeness could alone contrive.

Like most other endowments, Bhai Taru Singh's resting place has come to belong to hereditary keepers. It has a Jagir set apart for its maintenance; but both the Jagir and the offerings are appropriated by the keeper principally for his own private ends. With such a person to look after it, there is little wonder if the place should present a neglected appearance, and should be the least known and least visited.

Parenthetically it may be mentioned, that more than two decades back, when the writer happened to be temporarily living in Lahore, he made a serious effort to make the two Shahid Ganjs places of pilgrimage, so that the rising generation of the Sikhs might draw perennial inspiration from their brave co-religionists, whose heroic deeds had shed lustre on their past, and whose lofty examples might fill them with courage and hope for the future; but these and other activities came to all end with the writer's departure from Lahore. "The Khalsa," the first English organ of the Sikhs, that he had started with the help of a few friends and which was so enthusiastically received and supported, had also to stop publication. Similarly the movement that he had conceived of getting the Amritsar Khalsa College transferred to Lahore, and which had made a fair advance, had to be given up, along with several other useful plans for the amelioration of the community.

To return to Bhai Taru Singh. He was a resident of Poola in the Manjha *ilaqa*, now comprising the districts of Lahore and Amritsar. He was engaged in the peaceful occupation of agriculture, the proceeds of which he joyously shared with all who called at his abode, and sought shelter under his roof for a night's repose. The Khalsa at that time was under a ban. Men, women and children were sold and bartered. They were declared outlaws. Their heads were sold like those of tigers, wolves and snakes. The greed for reward, it is freely stated tempted their neighbours, Hindu and Mussalman alike, to cut off the heads of young damsels and pass them off as those of men professing the Khalsa faith. In these circumstances, it may be easily supposed that few would dare give shelter to the Khalsa; and those who did, did it at terrible risk. Of such rare souls was Bhai Taru Singh Somehow he had hitherto been allowed to live unmolested, and that in a populous village—a unique privilege. But he did not live long to enjoy social amenities. He is said to have incurred the enmity of one Bhagat Nirangni, a Khatri of his village. This man preferred a complaint against him to Khan Bahadur, Subah of Lahore, stating that Bhai Taru Singh harboured dacoits who spread havoc throughout the land, and that the lives and property of the Hindu and the Mussalman subjects of His Imperial Majesty were unsafe. As stated above, the lives of the Khalsa, under imperial edicts, were already in jeopardy. They were to be beheaded wherever and whenever caught. This being so, even a frivolous charge such as this was needless. The Subah ordered Bhai Taru Singh to be forthwith captured and brought before him. Bhai Taru Singh's followers offered resistance; but on the remonstrance of the Bhai, who did not like that the lives of his co-religionists should be sacrificed for him, they allowed him to be taken away. When asked to answer the charge brought against him, he plainly declared that he had given shelter to the Guru's followers, that he did not think he had done anything to be ashamed of and that he deemed it a privilege that the Guru, having given him plenty, had placed him in a position in which he could be of service to his co-religionists. This bold reply enraged the Subah. Without much ado, he ordered that Bhai Toru Singh's head be clean-shaven, which according to the tenets of the Khalsa was a sacrilege. Guru Govind Singh had for years invoked the 'Akal'[1] to grant him power to re-create the Rishis of yore, so that once again they might fight the battles of the Devas and free the holy Brahmarishi Desh—the country of Brahma Rishis—from the yoke of the Yavans. The prayer was granted and the world saw the great miracle wrought. Each and every follower of the tenth Guru became a Rishi—a power on the side of righteousness. On the banks of the sacred Sindhu, and

1. The Timeless One, the name by which Guru Govind Singh remembered the Creator.

her fair sisters the Devas again chanted Mantras[1] in praise of the great Creator of the Universe. From the spurs of the gold-crested Sumeru and the hoary Kailas. down to Dwaraka, and from the Kyber to remote Delhi, the places which had been made sacred by the touch of the holy feet of Rama and Lakshmana, Bharata and Satrughana, and of the illustrious Pandava brothers, during their long exile, were again restored to their owners. So the *keshas* (long hair) of a Khalsa were the *keshas* of the Rishis of old They were the emblem of all the glory that had attached for ages to the name Rishi. To part with the *keshas* was to part with this emblem, which reminded the Khalsa of their high origin, and of the lofty ideals which their noble progenitors had loved to live up to. Now Bhai Taru Singh was a true Khalsa, thoroughly imbued with the spirit of the age. He could not submit to the insult. The Subah's minions pinioned him and caught hold of his head and the chin; but the barber found it difficult to bring his hand near the Bhai. With

1. Hymns

one shake of his head, he would push back his assailants and make them whirl on the ground like so many tops. A shoemaker was then sent for, to try his skill with his tools and scraps off the Bhai's head; but he, too, proved a failure. At last the services of a carpenter were requisitioned for the fell deed. With one stroke of his adze, he cut off Bhai Taru Singh's head (1743 A.D.) which was triumphantly exhibited throughout the town.

Such was the heroic end of Bhai Turu Singh. His remains were cremated outside the Delhi Gate, Lahore, near the railway station. It is stated in the Sikh chronicles that immediately after Bhai Taru Singh died, the Subah got a severe attack of kidney pain. He could not pass urine, and his abdomen swelled till breathing became difficult. This visitation he attributed to his unrighteous persecution of Bhai Taru Singh. He sent messengers to the Khalsa asking for forgiveness. For a time, the Khalsa had some respite and were allowed to return to their homes. But although the Subah's pain ceased, he died soon after from other complications.

CHAPTER XV

SARDAR SUBEG SINGH AND SHAHBAZ SINGH

Sardar Subeg Singh, a resident of Jhambar, a village a few miles from Lahore, was Kotwal of Lahore. He had risen to this position by unusual ability and integrity. During his tenure of office, Lahore enjoyed peace and tranquility not known for years Hence he was deservedly popular both with his official superiors and the people. He had a son, Shahbaz Singh, aged 18 years, who was placed under the tutelage of bigoted Mullah. Born of respectable parents, Shahbaz was unusually handsome, and he was a bright and promising boy. The teacher took, a fancy to him and began to contrive means for his conversion to the Islamic creed, with a view to marry his daughter to him. By an artful admixture of threats and cajolery he strove to hoodwink the boy ; but failed in his attempt. Though young in years, Shahbaz Singh was well informed on comparative religious philosophy. His subtle reasoning and slashing arguments struck at the very root of the beliefs, which the Mullah and his fellow-thinkers cherished and thought so highly of.

All fondness for the boy was now gone. The devil of vindictiveness possessed the Mullah so completely that he bent all the energy of his soul on the lad's destruction. He approached the Kazi of Lahore, a notorious blood-thirsty tyrant, and sought his assistance. But to no avail. Shahbaz was inexorable. Nothing could tempt or frighten him. All endeavours having failed, the astute Mullah led by the blood-thirsty magistrate, implored the help of Yahya Khan Subah of Lahore, son of the notorious Khan Bahadur. Yahya Khan sent for the boy's father, and forgetting his distinguished services, accused him of holding seditious opinions, and plainly told him that, unless both he and his son embraced Islam their life and property would be forfeited. This sudden change in the attitude of his official superior no doubt came upon Sardar Subeg Singh as a great surprise; but he was a highly cultured Khalsa, possessed of devout disposition and an iron will. He had a firm faith in the well-known words of the holy scripture which taught that this life was only a preparation for the life eternal He had lived well and deserved well. Confident, therefore, of happiness in the world to come, he found no difficulty in giving a bit of his mind to the Subah. He challenged his traducers to name any act, overt or covert, which could be taken as hostile to his sovereign or to the creed of Islam. He referred to a host of incidents in his life which bore testimony to his public spirit and cosmopolitan sympathy. As regards Shahbaz, he said that he knew him to be quite innocent, and that if he had said anything derogatory to Islam, it must have been due to the fanatical Mullah's injuring the lad's feelings and provoking the remarks complained of. The Subah was all fire and fury. When did the Turk ever listen to reason? Forthwith orders were issued for the arrest of both the father and the son They were incarcerated in different prisons, and subjected to unspeakable tortures. Day after day, they were brought before the Subah. Hopes of rewards in this world and the next were held out to them in case they embraced Islam. Threats of most terrible forms of death were given in case of refusal. But all this was of no avail. The noble father and the brave boy held fast to their beliefs, and manfully faced the cruellest of deaths. At length the assassins led out the brave martyrs, placed them on the wheel and crushed them to pieces (1748 A. D.)

The intelligence of the horrid deed spread like wild-fire. The majority of the Moslems looked askance. A few thought that matters were going too far. The Hindus had become paralysed. But the few whose hearts still pulsated with love, to howsoever small an extent, shed tears of sympathy. The Khalsa infuriated with rage, came out of their haunts in remote fastnesses and spread over the land like locusts, wreaking vengeance on the tyrants and their sympathisers and supporters, and sparing not a vestige of what they held dear. This done, they went back to their retreats. The turbulent part of the Turk population was cooled down a little, and the peacefully inclined people of all phases of belief cursed, in their hearts the men whose evil genius had given uncalled for provocation to the Khalsa, and had thus brought on them so much woe and misery. Thus, quite unconsciously, the tyrannical rulers were losing their hold over the affections of the subject population. They were contributing to their own destruction and hastening the advent of the Khalsa rule. Virtue, as a common saying goes, is its own reward. Inversely, villainous conduct as sure as anything, leads but to perdition, however, much men may indulge in self-deception, seeking justification for their subservience to the devil within them.

Though the mills of God grind slowly,
  Yet He grinds exceedingly small ;
Though with patience stands He waiting,
  With exactness grinds He all.

CHAPTER XVI

THE FIRST HOLOCAUST A WHOLE PEOPLE SACRIFICED

The foregoing are only a few instances of individuals who received martyrdom for loyalty to their creed or coun ry, who preferred honourable death to life without honour, and who were more or less persons of consequence, known to the community and the Government of the day. This is why their names are chronicled, and their deeds are remembered by friends and foes alike. But the miscreants, who held in their hands the reins of power, were thirsting for the blood of the whole Khalsa people. They did not stop here. They had a "Gashti Fauj",—itinerant army, as they called it,—whose primary duty was police work. It was now requisitioned for the harassment of the entire Sikh population and, what is particularly noteworthy, in not a few cases, it were the Hindus who were the principal instigators. The Mussalman rulers were hoodwinked into the belief by their clever, intriguing Hindu ministers that the creed of the Khalsa was anti-Moslem, and that its progress meant the downfall of the Moslem power. It will be easily understood, therefore that the Moslem rulers, whose overzeal for their creed is always so marked, lent a willing ear to the representations of their crafty Hindu agents. And, as all that was done was, ostensibly, done in the name of the Moslem, the quarrel took the form of a Khalsa-Moslem quarrel. Men forgot who the real instigators were and, in their exasperation, the ire of their wrath fell chiefly on the Mussalman.

In the foregoing pages, mention has been made of Chandu, an officer of some note, in Lahore, who was principally instrumental in the torture and death of Guru Arjan Dev. Again, it was Sucha Nand Khatri, the Hindu Minister of Bazid Khan, Subah of Sirhind, at whose instance Princes Zorawar Singh and

Fateh Singh, mere children then were bricked up alive. It must be said to the credit of Bazid Khan that he, personally, did not favour the idea of spilling the blood of the innocent children. Much more accursed is the memory of the brothers Jaspat Rai and Lakhpat Rai, Khatris of Eminabad, in the Gujranwalla district. Lakhpat was the Prime Minister of Zakraya Khan, Subah of Lahore, and Jaspat held charge of the districts of Sialkot and Gujranwalla besides being also Secretary to his brother. Both were ultra-loyal, out and out hypocrites who, though Hindus in name, were more pro-Moslems than Moslems themselves. Their attitude towards the Khalsa and the Khalsa propaganda were hostile in the extreme, and they were most unrelenting. The home of the Khalsa was in those days on the saddle The rulers of the day had made it impossible for them to think of breathing the air of human habitations, or seeing a human face in the day-light. Even sojourn in jungles was made too hot for them, literally and metaphorically. These were set fire to, so that they might not afford shelter to the Khalsa. Hence, the Khalsa was always on the move. Once, a small party of Sikhs halted at Rorhi Sahib, in the vicinity of Eminabad, with a view to have a look at the local Gurdwara, sacred to the memory of Baba Nanak. When Jaspat Rai, who was then at his native place, came to know of it, he forthwith made for the Khalsa camp and demanded the immediate evacuation of the place. The Khalsa leaders remonstrated at this interference; but to on avail. The very face of the Khalsa was, to this parasite of the Turk rulers of the day, a hateful sight. The loathsome vituperations he indulged in, exasperated the party, one of whom shot the man in the forehead and thus put an end to his existence Jaspat's companions fled with his remains to Eminabad, and the party of the Khalsa wended its way northward. The rowdies of the place saw their opportunity. Their rapacity was aroused, and they lost no time in taking the law into their own hands. Eminabad was pillaged and plundered, and the rich kinsmen of Jaspat and Lakhpat were relieved of the treasures which they had hoarded for generations.

When Lakhpat was apprised of the incident, he was naturally shocked and vowed terrible vengeance. Had he been a fair-minded man he would have tried to find out the real culprits and bring them to book. But he was an ill-bred, grasping, greedy tyrant, more a boa-constrictor than man, whom nothing but the blood of the whole people professing the Khalsa faith could satisfy. He soon approached his master, Zakraya Khan, Subah of Lahore,—a son of Abdul Samad Khan who had captured Banda the Brave and his valiant companions, had them disgraced in Lahore and butchered in Delhi in the most atrocious manner. Like father, like son. Zakraya felt no scruple or compunction in the matter. Forthwith, he issued a proclamation "for general massacre of all Sikhs, wherever they could be found, Death was to be the punishment of all persons who invoked the name of Guru Govind Singh and reward was offered for the heads of Sikhs. Thousands were put to death daily, and their heads brought before the Subadar of Lahore for reward."[1] The result of this proclamation was that those of the Khalsa who either did not like to be involved in a quarrel with the Government of the day, or who thought that they were not equal to the task, deserted their homes and betook themselves to the jungles. Even here they were hunted from piller to post, until they took shelter in a dense bush near Kahnowan Lake in the district of Gurdaspur, and there stood at bay to face their relentless foe.

When the Israelites found it difficult to live in the land of the Pharaohs, they went on a voluntary exile under the leadership of their heavenly-appointed guide and friend, Moses, who worked miracles to ensure the safe arrival of his following in the hospitable land of Canaan. When the English Non Conformists, called the Pilgrim Fathers, felt compelled to did good-bye to their kith and kin at home, and sailed away in the "Mayflower," to seek in the virgin lands across the Atlantic the freedom of

---

1 History of the Punjab by Sayaed Mohd Latif. P. 213.

conscience, which was denied to them in their own country, their persecutors, no doubt, heaved a sigh of relief and felt jubilant; but there were others both in England and elsewhere, who sympathized with them in their troubles, and held them up to the admiring gaze of the world as patriotic adventures, who had set an example of enterprise and sacrifice and laid in distant America the foundations of the Greater Britain. Only two years ago when as a result of the Khilafat agitation, the Mussalmans of India left in their hundreds, by way of protest against the attitude of England towards the Khilafat question, to find a home in Afghanistan and its borders, the Government of India not only showed no resentment at this parade of disaffection, but actually restored the immovable property of those disillusioned zealots who had subsequently to return like the Prodigal Son, and even helped them with large amounts of subsidies to put them on their legs again.

But no Jehova promised a land of milk and honey to the Khalsa, and no Moses offered himself as a guide to them. They were not going in quest of an *El Dorado*: but in search of a place where they could breathe God's free air and enjoy some sort of immunity from the hands of their cruel persecutors. But this was a consideration which carried no weight with Lakhpat and his patrons. There have been men who thought that the ends of justice could be met only by taking a tooth for a tooth and an eye for an eye or who, like Shylock, would be satisfied with nothing less than the stipulated pound of flesh. There have also been men who believed that it was a gross sin even to think of retaliation. In the Bible, for instance, Christ enjoins upon his follows to turn their left cheek to the good people who might take it into their head to strike them on their right one. In the Sikh scriptures, too, such a conduct is held up as exemplary; and, though, it may be safely said that there have not been many men, belonging to either of these dispensations, who have seriously thought of transplating such punctilious ethical maxims into practice, yet it is not uncommon occurrence to find men who take into consideration the extenuating circumstances, and pardon men guilty even of wilful murder. Unfortunately, however, at the head of affairs in the Punjab, at the time, were men, who considered the assassination of one official as a sufficient excuse for ordering the indiscriminate slaughter of hundreds of thousands of innocent men, women and children. The most that was required was to get hold of the assassin or assassins responsible for Jaspat Rai's premature end, and make an example of them. But Lakhpat and his Turk patrons would be satisfied with nohting short of the total destructions of the whole Khalsa people.

The struggle was obviously very unequal. The Mussalman forces numbering more than a lac of trained veterans and consisting, in part, of fanatics drawn from all over the country, outnumbered the Khalsa by one to five, They were, withal, well-provisioned and well-supplied with munition and the latest weapons of war. The Khalsa, on the other hand, were armed with cudgels and the crudest weapons. Still they gave a good account of themselves. The enemy had set fire to the bush. All exits on the other side, were flanked by the huge masses of enemy battalions. The only way of escape was to cut through the ranks of the enemy, regardless of consequences. This was done One night, under cover of darkness the Khalsa cut a passage for themselves and made their way to the hills in the belief that they would fare better there But their old foe, the hillsmen, and their chieftains blocked all ingress into their territory. The Khalsa were, therefore, completed to halt on the spurs of the mountains of Basohli and to offer battle. With the enemy behind them, high precipitous mountains to the north and west of them, peopled by a hostile population, and with the Beas to the right of them, the Khalsa were in a sad predicament. The fight was desperate. Lakhpat's men fell upon the Khalsa like enraged tigers. The cries of "Allah-o-Akbar." and "Sat Sri Akal" rent the air. The dead lay in heaps upon heaps, and blood flowed in torrents. Both sides lost heavily. Har Bhaj, Lakpat's nephew, and Nahar Khan and Saif Ali Khan, the Turk Commanders;

fell in the action. Himmat Beg, another Turk chief, took to heels. The cowardly Lakhpat saved his skin by hiding. The loss of the Khalsa was, however, tremendous, and they rightly called this action as *Ghallu Ghara* an indiscriminate slaughter in an open field. Of about 22,000 Sikhs, who took part in the action only about 10,000 escaped to the Sutlej. There they obtained respite and had time to attend their injured and wounded.

Lakhpat was,perhaps, under the impression that he had exterminated the Khalsa[1] and that all trouble was at an end. Like the hydra-headed monster, Raktbij of the Indian mythology, whom the gods favoured, and who received several new heads whenever he chanced to lose one, the Khalsa were not only able

1. According to S. Mohammad Latif, "to complete his revenge, Lakhpat Rai brought with him 1,000 Sikhs in irons to Lahore, and having compelled them to ride on donkeys bare-backedi paraded them in the bazars. They were, than, taken to the horse-market, outside t Delhi Gate, and there beheaded one after another withe out mercy." (History of the Punjab, P. 213).

to recoup themselves, they soon increased ten-fold in number, all burning with religious zeal and yearning for opportunities to wreak vengeance not only on the cruel heartless Turks, but also on the accomodating, perfidious Hindus, and, even the so-called professed Sikhs who acted as spies and served as willing tools of oppression in the hands of the Turks.

Lakhpat himself came to an ignominious and a very sad end, and thereby hangs a tale. The infamous Zakraya Khan, Yahya Khan's father who had grown fat by the plunder of the Khalsa Protestants, died without making a proper bequest. Yahya Khan, who succeeded him in the viceroyalty of Lahore, appropriated everything to himself. His brother, Shah Nawaz Governor of Multan, came to Lahore and demanded his share of the property. Yahya Khan refused to give anything. The result was an action, fought between both brothers on the grounds of the Shalamar Gardens, where Shah Nawaz had encamped. Yahya Khan was taken prisoner together with his Minister, Lakhpat. The Satrapy of Lahore also fell to the share of Shah Nawaz Yahya Khan escaped from the jail and fled to Delhi, where he took shelter with the Vizir. Qamar-ud-Din his uncle and father-in-law. The latter wrote threateningly to Shah Nawaz asking him to restore the viceroyalty of Lahore to Yahya Khan. At the same time he despatched a detachment of the Imperial Force to Lahore under the command of his son. Mir Muin-ul-Mulk, better known as Mir Mannu whose hated name will always remain associated with the Khalsa history. Shah Nawaz, forthwith, invited Ahmad Shah Abdali of Kabul to come and take possession of the Punjab. Nothing could be more welcome to the latter, who lost no time in reaching Lahore. When Vizir Qamar-ud-Din heard of this, both he and the Emperor were filled with alarm. They thought it wise to make up with Shah Nawaz and recognise him as Subah of Lahore. Shah Nawaz was asked to oppose the Abdali and simultaneously preparations were made for marching an Imperial Force to oppose his progress On receipt of these orders Shah Nawaz took up a hostile attitude towards the Abdali. The latter exasperated beyond description, at once laid siege to Lahore, and captured it after a brief action. Lakhpat, whose kinsmen had betrayed Shah Nawaz, and had helped in his defeat, was released from his captivity and was granted the Satrapy of Lahore in place of Shah Nawaz, who had fled to Delhi, as a reward for the services of his family. This done, the Abdali marched to Delhi. At Sirhind, a battle took place between his forces and those of the Imperial Delhi, under the command of the Heir-Apparent Ahmed Shah, and Vizir Qamar-ud-Din. The forces of the Abdali suffered a serious defeat and he was compelled to retrace his footsteps to Kabul. His namesake of Delhi appointed Muin-ul-Mulk, the hated Mannu, Viceroy of Lahore. Mannu sent Lakhpat again to jail, where he came to a terrible end, 1750 A.D., the details of which are too shocking to mention. Suffice it to say that thousands of bereaved parents, whose sons and daughters he had so cruelly tortured to death, thought it an act of merit to visit him in the jail and bespatter him with filth. His property was forfeited to the State and his whole family incurred public obloquy.

CHAPTER XVII

TURANIAN ATROCITIES

The code of ethics which the Turk rulers followed, preculded all feelings of chivalry. They believed only in inspiring awe, and there was no measure, however reprehensible, that they did not consider lawful to adopt in exterminating the whole Sikh race. Though it was the State that was originally responsible for initiating this policy;the prominent share in the persecution of the Sikhs fell to the lot of a Turani noble, Abdul Samad Khan, *Diler Jang*, Viceroy of Kashmir, his son Zakraya Khan, surnamed Khan Bahadur, his grandson, Yahya Khan,and another grandson Mir Muin-ul-Mulk, surnamed Mir Mannu, all of whom became Viceroys of Lahore,one after the other. To quote Sayed Mohammad Latif again, "Abdul Samad Khan, having humiliated the Sikhs and caused the destruction of their leader,Banda, now took vigorous steps to destroy their power and extirpate the race. A royal edict was issued to put all who professed the religion of Nanak to the sword, and a money reward was offered for the head of every Sikh. The irritated Mohammadans gave them no quarter, and wherever a Sikh was found he was butchered mercilessly. In order to give fuel effect to the royal mandate, Mohammadans and Hindus were strictly enjoined to clip their hair short. The Hindus were ordered to shave their beards, and any Hindu found with long beards,or hair,was immediately slain." (History of the Punjab, p. 188).

"Zakrya Khan offered munificent rewards for the arrest of notorious Sikh robbers and plunderers,and they were daily brought in chains and executed in the streets of Lahore. These vigorous measures had the desired effect. Peace and tranquility reigned in the Punjab. The Sikhs were completely vanquished and were not to be seen even in Manjha, the country chiefly inhabited by them." (Ibid p. 193).

Thus, evidently the whole Sikh population

was dealt with as if it consisted of robbers and plunderers. Even women and children were treated as dacoits. Manjha was cleared of all Sikhs and was transplanted by Hindus and Mohammans. But what do we see now? Manjha is wholly Sikh and the people are all Jats. Zakraya Khan's massacres were all in vain. Only the memory of his dark deeds is all that is left of him. Sayed Mohammad Latif continues: "On the death of Zakraya Khan, his eldest son, Yahya Khan, was appointed Governor, through the good offices of his maternal grand-father-in-law, Vizir Qamar-ud-Din. Soon after his succession, he issued a proclamation for a general massacre of all Sikhs, wherever they could be found. Death was to be the punishment of all persons who invoked the name of Guru Govind Singh, and a reward was offered for the heads of the Sikhs. Thousands were put to death daily, and their heads brought before the Subadar of Lahore for the reward. As usual with the votaries of the Guru on such occasions, many had their long hair cut short and their flowing beards clipped to avoid detection and consequent death; while others concealed themselves in the jungles or fled across the Sutlej." (*Ibid*, p. 213)

It was not long before Yahya Khan also had to pay the penalty of his crimes. A family quarrel resulted in his being ousted from the Lahore Satrapy by his brother Shah Nawaz Khan, who put Yahya Khan and Lakhpat Rai in confinement and began to rule the Punjab with the help of his Minister, Diwan Kaura Mal. The Khalsa had now a respite, but Vizir Qamar ud-Din would not allow the peaceful Shah Nawaz to assume the goverment. Thereupon Shah Nawaz invited Ahmad Shah Abdali to come and take possession of the Punjab,a request which that ambitious monarch was only too glad to accept; but he soon found that he had been betrayed. What transpired subsequently, has been related in the previous chapter. When,at last,the Abdali went back to Kabul, the Viceroyalty of Lahore was conferred on Mir Mannu. The first act of this monster was 'to storm the fort of Ram Rauni which he captured and reduced. He then stationed detachments of troops in all parts populated by the Sikhs with stringent orders to shave their heads and beards wherever they might be found.. ... Mir Mannu issued strict orders to the Hill Rajas to seize the Sikhs and send them in irons to Lahore. These orders were obeyed and hundreds of Sikhs were brought daily to Lahore and butchered at the Nakhas, or Shahid Gunj, outside the Delhi Gate, in sight of multitudes of spectators. The young Mannu became an irreconcilable foe of the Sikhs and was determined to extirpate the nation." (*Ibid* p. 221.) No wonder, therefore, that, to use the words of Sayed Mohammad Latif, the memory of Mannu is "detested," by the Sikhs. Sayed Mohammad Latif ruefully remarks that "the last resting place of the once draded Governor of Lahore is now occupied by wine-merchants (Gurdit Singh & Co.)"–not a strange comment on the ultimate nothingnesss of worldly glory !

When all other sources of persecution were exhausted and the raides of the Khalsa from their hiding places continued to be as frequent as every it suggested itself to the hated Mannu that the capture of the women and children of the Khalsa would force them to leave their places of shelter and seek an open battle in which, thought he, the Khalsa would be completely decimated on account of their lack of discipline and ammunition. With the previous approval of the Delhi Governmment, he promised the grant of Jagirs and handsome rewards to all who would capture the women and children of the Khalsa and hand them over to the authorities. There was a hearty response. Men, who had hitherto wavered in their loyalty to the Government now thought it well worth their while to completely identify themselves with it. All toadies and parasites, who invariably surround the powers that be, expressed their hearty approval of the new policy. It offered them an excellent opportunity of making name and fame as also of adding to the coffees a few more pieces of silver and gold, though soiled by the blood of the innocent people of the country which had given them birth,—nay, even of those who were related to them by the sacred ties of kinship and religion. To Patwaries,

Zaildars and Lamberdars, and to the village Sahukars, who love to fawn on the rulers of the day, this was a grand opportunity. Before long, every petty and big official had collected a swarm of Sikh men, women and children, and their headquarters were converted into slaughter-houses, where the poor captives were flayed and, not unoften, burnt alive.

The Turk rulers, Maulvis, and Kazis had a grotesque idea of propriety. While thus engaged in ruthless slaughter, they invariably showed great partiality for young women, whom they would leave no stone unturned to possess. The Sikh chronicles all say that Mannu made frantic appeals to the women captives to accept Islam, and enjoy the peace and happiness of this world and the beatitude of the next;but not one paid heed to his overtures. These overtures were followed by threats which were given practical effect to. For instance, children were snatched from the breasts of their mothers, and thrown into the space like so many balls, to fall at last to the ground and be dashed to pieces. But even then the ladies spurned the offers of the profligate Mannu, and of his no less savage underlings, with unflinching courage. Their wail went up the sky, and it was not long before their prayer was heard, and the Almighty God, that father of all innocent and weak people, came to their rescue.

A strong detachment of the Khalsa appeared on the scene. The Khalsa ladies were rescued and escorted to their homes. The informers officials and jagirdars who had helped in the arrest of the ladsies were caught hold of, and were all put to the sword. Nur-ud-Din's serai was burnt and pulled down. The Turks of Pathankot, the Jat informers of Majitha, and Mahant Akil Das of Jandiala, were similarly chastised Karma Chinna, with his whole family, was called to account and punished. The villages of Rama and Kanahya were similarly dealt with. Sayedwala was plundered and its principal citizen, Dayala, a Government man, was put to death. Nawahu of Bhurewal, Ismail of Jandiala, the Sidhu Jats of Bundala, and the Ranghars of Batala met the same fate. Aulia Khan of Pindi Gheb, Hassan

Khan Bhatti, and Gulaba of Mahilpur, were treated in the same way.

News now arrived of Mannu's premature end. He met with a riding accident and lost his life This occurred in 1756 A.D. It was hoped that with his disappearance from the scene there would be a change in the repressive and oppressive policy of the Lahore Government; especially as there was now a woman at the head of affairs. But these expectations were not realized. Murad Begum, Mannu's widow, who ruled in the name of her infant son, was found only too faithful in the discharge of the legacy left to her by her husband. She was easily able to find the right sort of person in Moman Khan of Kasur, under whom the policy of repression was again in full swing. A clever adept in the intrigues of the Lahore Court, and lost to all sense of honour, there was nothing which this man would not do to gain his end. He placed himself at the head of the "Gashti Fauj", and ordered the ruthless massacre of the women and children of the Khalsa who had escaped to the hills and forests. No Sikh village or hamlet, escaped his attention, and there was no crime which he did not commit. A revolution in the Lahore Court made the state of things still more acute.

Murad Begum had a beautiful daughter, whose hand was sought by Ghazi-ud-Din- the Delhi Vizir. The Vizir's overtures were, however, repulsed, upon which he marched on Lahore, deprived the widow of her rank and liberty and married her daughter by force. The Begum, then, went to Kabul and personally sought help from Ahmad Shah Abdali. In reponse to this appeal, the Abdali came and engaged the Imperial forces at Lahore, and having driven them out,he garrisoned the place with his own men, leaving his son, Timur, in their charge, with Jahan Khan as his assistant. The campaign against the Sikhs was again started with full force. "The Sikh stronghold at Amritsar, called the Ram Rauni, was attacked and levelled with the ground. The sacred reservior was filled up, and all their places of worship were defiled. This outrage on the scared city of the Khalsa provoked the whole

Sikh nation to such a degree that they assembled in great numbers, and determined to defend their religion with the sword. They ravaged the whole country round Lahore, which swarmed with Sikh horsemen. Jahan Khan came against them and succeeded at first in dispersing them. The Sikhs, however, assembled in large number and were strong enough not only to cut off communication between the fort and the country, but also to collect the revenues of the country around Lahore, and dispose of it as they liked. The Afghan prince engaged them on several occasions, but was worsted each time in consequence of the superiority of their numbers. In a desperate engagement which took place between the Afghans and the Sikhs, the Pathans were completely routed, and this was the first decisive victory on record achieved by the Sikhs over the Afghans. The Afghan prince and his guardian, seeing that all their attempts to disperse the Sikhs had failed, and that the numbers of the insurgents were daily increasing by thousands, considered it prudent to evacuate Lahore. They retreated in the night unknown even to their Hindustani troops whom they distursted. The truimphant Sikhs occupied Lahore under their celebrated leader, Jassa, Kalal, who now assumed the sovereignty of the country.'' (History of the Punjab, by Sayed Mohammad Latif, P. 230).

Once Nawab Kapur Singh sitting in the midst of his gallant comrades in the forest remarked how good it would be if an intrepid Khalsa brought him the head of the miscreant Moman. Aghar Singh, a brave youth, who was one of the assembly, offered his services for the purpose. Moman Khan was always in fear for his life and went about properly escorted. So Aghar Singh's task was by no means an easy one. But he was a man of resolute purpose, and, once he had made up his mind to do a thing, nothing in the world could daunt him. He took up the guise of a Mughal to be able to prowl about freely. One evening when the Khan was out for a walk. Aghar Singh sprang upon him from behind a bush, and hallooed to him to defend himself. The Khan was taken aback, his attendants deserted him and he fell an easy prey to the blow of his assailant. Aghar Singh cut off his head, brought it to the rendezvous of the Khalsa in triumph, and received the blessings of the whole party. (1757 A D.)

The Khalsa had now only one foe left in the person of Adina Beg Khan, a cunning, cruel and unprincipled adventure. On occasions, he had assisted the Khalsa with view to weaken the power of the Afghan masters of the Punjab and take possession of the province himself; but when he found that Khalsa were too strong for him, he resolved upon destroying the whole of their race root and branch. The opportunity soon presented itself to him. When Prince Timur and his General, Jahan Khan, suffered defeat and vacated Lahore. the Khalsa under the leadership of Sardar Jassa Singh Ahluwalia took possession of it. Adina Beg's agent, Mirza Jan had, of course, to go. This was a severe blow to his ambition. In a fit of rage, he inivited the Mahrattas who had, then, made themselves virtual masters of Delhi, to come and take possession of the Punjab. The invitation was at once accepted. An engagement took place outside Lahore with prince Timur and his General, Jahan Khan, in which the Afghans sustained a defeat. The victorious Mahratta troops entered Lahore and turned on the Sikhs and, as a reward for his services, Adina Beg Khan was appointed viceroy. It was then that he conceived the project of extirpating the Khalsa. To quote Sayed Mohammad Latif again, "Mir Aziz Bakshi, in command of a strong body of cavalry, was sent to the Manjha country with orders to attack and chastise the Sikhs wherever they could be found. Four thousand pioneers accompanied the Mir with their sharpened tools for the purpose of clearing the jungles where the Sikhs had concealed themselves. Thousands of Sikhs were thus hunted down and butchered." (History of the Punjab, p. 307.) But the Adina Beg Khan was not destined to rule over the Punjab for any length of time. Like the will-of-the wisp, the viceroyalty again slipped from his hands as soon as it came to him. The Rohilas mutinied against him. The Malerkotlia Afghans also raised the standard of revolt. The insurgents were defeated; but the Khalsa again rose on all sides. Adina was preparing to face them, when he was taken ill and died, 1757 A.D. This is what Syed Mohammad Latif says of him:— "He was a master of Indian diplomacy. The Sikhs he amused; the Delhi Court he despised; the Afghans he bewildered; and the Mahrattas he effectively influenced in his favour to break the power of both Sikhs and Afghans and obtain to his own advantage. He was unscrupulous and somewhat cruel. Once he ordered a confectioner, who had refused to supply him with preserves, to be boiled alive." (History of the Punjab, p.232)

CAAPTER XVIII

THE ABDALI EXHAUSTS HIMSELF

When the Mahrattas wrested Delhi from Najib-ud-Daulah, the latter invited Ahmad Shah Durrani from Kabul to come and oust them. A battle was fought between the Afghan forces and the Mahrattas, in which the latter sustained a heavy defeat. They lost a hundred thousand men, apart from crores of rupees and fifty thousand horses, which fell into the hands of the Abdali. The number of Hindu women taken captives was 20,000. When the brave Khalsa learnt that so many Hindus ladies[1] were being carried off, they fell upon the Afghan forces near Govindwal. The women were released from the hand of their captors and sent to their respective homes. The greater part of the treasure that was seized was distributed and appropriated for various objects of public usefulness. When Ahmad Shah heard this at Lahore, he became furiously enraged. Sarbuland Khan, Kabuli, was appointed Governor of Multan and entrusted with the work of destroying the Khalsa. This man deputed Surat Singh, Rajput, an employee of Adina Beg Khan, Subah of Jullandhar, to do this unpleasant work for him. Surat Singh proving unequal to the task, Amir Mohammad was sent to replace him. He, too, was unable to do much. Karimdad Khan, Subah of Lahore, similarly came in for his share of obloquy, and was replaced by Hamid Khan. This done, Ahmad Shah continued his march to Kabul No sooner had he crossed the Indus, the Khalsa spread over the land once more. All tale-bearers and their accomplices were caught and put to death. Kalanaur was plundered and its chief, Hassan Khan, was slain. Sialkct was invaded and Shah Beg, a son of the official who had arrested Haqiqat Rai, as also the perfidious Kazis and Maulanas, who had so cruelly condemned him to death, were all put to the sword. The towns of Wazirabad, Gujrat and Jalalpur Jattan were besieged, and not one Turk chief, who failed to give a satisfactory account of himself was left alive.

Ahmad Shah, on his part, had not forgotten the insult to his arms. Immediately on his arrival in Kabul, he sent Nur-ud-din and Zalim Khan; at the head of seven thousands Ghilzais, with orders to destroy the Khalsa root and branch. Sardar Charat Singh of Gujranwalla grandfather of Maharaja Ranjit Singh, went forward to oppose the progress of Nur-ud din, who suffered a defeat and fled to Sialkot, concealing himself there. The Khalsa laid siege to this place; but Nur-ud-Din made his escape to Jammu, under cover of a dark night, and took shelter with Raja Ranjit Deo. At Sialkot a great quantity of provisions and ammunition fell into the hands of the Khalsa, who soon after returned to Gujranwalla where they built the first kutcha fortress for themselves. Hamid Khan came from Lahore to pull down the fortress, but the Khalsa ran from all over the country to the aid of Sardar Charat Singh. Hamid Khan retreated to Lahore, leaving several pieces of cannon in the hands of the Khalsa. Thus was laid the foundation-stone of the government of the Khalsa.

Like the ill-starred Nadir, Ahmad Shah, too, knew no rest. Like him, too, he became a notorious free-booter. But he was not destined to be the ruler of a vast empire, though he burnt with that ambition. He had wrested the Punjab from Mohammad Shah under the belief that it would be as easy to hold as any other Indian province. Like all despots possessed of illimitable power, he underrated the magnitude and the importance of the spirit that pervaded the Sikh Punjab, and he thought that it was an easy task to crush this spirit. With this aim, therefore, he wrote to his agents in the Punjab to try by all means in their power to put an end to the existence of this strange, turbulent people. Zen Khan from Sirhind, Sarbuland Khan from Multan, Nur-ud-Din, Zalim Khan, Mir Mohammad and Moman Khan met at Lahore, the Subah of which place joined them, in taking a concerted action against the Khalsa. In the neighbourhood of the town of Patti, a great battle took place between the consolidated army of the Turk rulers and the undisciplined Khalsa irregulars. It was an unequal contest. The Khalsa suffered a repulse and took shelter in far-off hills and forests, where they eked out a most miserable existence. The villages were all picketed by Imperial men, and the Khalsa found therein were liable to be arrested and beheaded. Hence they had to shift for themselves in the jungles and subsist upon what food they could get there During the day, they concealed themselves in bushes and caverns, and during the night, they had damp marshes for their beds, or the branches of tall trees to perch upon.

Such hardy, selfless men were not easy to deal with. The search parties of the relentless rulers, failing to lay hold of male members of the houses they visited, set fire to the dwellings and put old men, old women and children to the sword. Young women were, however, taken captives and were huddled together like flocks of sheep and goats, in cabined, cribbed and confined houses, where they could not even get

God's free air to breathe. All means were employed to force them to accept the creed of Islam, but both cajolery and force proved of little value. The Sikh ladies remained firmed as rock, and would rather die than give up their faith. When necessary, they even used force to keep off their beastly tyrants. This happened throughout the province. The story of the Sikh ladies of Pindauri, near Miran Kot, would serve as an illustration.

Finding life in the village insecure, the ladies thought it comparatively safe to take shelter in Saint Dandu Ram's hermitage, an out-of-the way place, some distance from the village. Mir Mohammad, the Lahore Commander, was supervising the espionage work of the itinerant Government forces stationed in the vicinity. When information reached him of the escape of the Khalsa ladies, he, forthwith, started for the locality. Espying from some distance the clouds of dust from the Lahore side, the good Dandu apprehended that it must be due to the forced marches of Turk Gashti Fauj (itinerant army). Immediately he arranged to hide the ladies in sugarcane fields close by. The chagrin of the cruel Turks knew no bounds when they saw the whole place empty. The hermit was subjected to nameless tortures to compel him to give information as to the whereabouts of the ladies, but the brave man remained quite obdurate. In despair, the miscreants were returning to Lahore, when the stifled cries of babies, who were naturally frightened in their hiding places, disclosed the secrct. With a truimphant shout, the cruel desperadoes ran to the spot, dragged out the ladics and marched them to Patti, where they were incarcerated. Meanwhile the news of the arrest of their ladies reached the Khalsa in their hiding places, and aroused their chivalrous feelings. By forced marches, they took the Turk forces by surprise and routed them. The miscreant, Mir Mohammad, who had never felt pity or remorse in his ruthless campaign against the Khalsa, was paid in his own coin. He was caught while flying to Lahore, and, forthwith, beheaded, his body being cremated then and there. This was done to strike terror into the heart of the Turk oppressors for, according to their belief, men whose bodies are consumed by cremation, straightway go to hell.

Incidents like this only served to stiffen the resistance of the Khalsa, until the time came when it was no longer possible for the Turks to ignore Sikh influence in the Punjab. They were, then led to feel that their own safety lay, first, in adopting a policy of conciliation towards the Khalsa, and, later, in offering complacent submission to them, when the Khalsa became the suzerain power.

This is not the moral only of the story of the Khalsa. History is full of instances in which men have hoisted themselves with their own petard. No end of Turks filled the graves which they had dug for the Khalsa. Alas ! men do not see how transitory are the things of this earth for which they daily despoil their fellow-beings of their birthright, regardless of all sense of honour and dictates of justice. Places of worship are erected with domes -high; but it is the Mammon who is worshipped therein and not the Most High.

How beautifully does the blessed Christ call on his followers to turn their left cheek also to whosoever smites their right one, to give their cloak also to any one who sues them for a coat to love their enemies, to bless those that curse them, and pray for those who use them "despitefully;" so that they might deserve to be called the children of the "Father which is in heaven," for He maketh His sun to shine on the evil and on the good, and sendeth rain on the just and the unjust." In exactly the same strain; Guru Govind Singh sings of the solicitude of the Creator for His created objects. Says he: - "Why shouldst thou, O man, disturb the peace of thy mind ? The illustrious Lord of the Lotus Feet maketh generous provision for all things, living or without life, in all places and at all times. He cherishes thee in his mind for ever and ever." But, alas, where are the Christians who follow these sublime maxims ? Where are the Mussalmans who actually treat

1. Jan ko det ajain ko det, zamin ko det zaman ko de hai.

Kahe ko dolat hain, tumri sudh Sri Padmapat aphi le hai.

all men as their own brothers ? Where are the men who will not think of the morrow ? Where and how many are there who have faith in the Guru and believe that God will send them what they need, and that it is a sin for them to think of riches, not to speak of hoarding them ? And yet it will have to be conceded that the only true way in which the Kingdom of God can be established in this world is the way which has been shown by Jesus Christ and Nanak, nay, by all the true and great men of all nations of the earth and of all ages.

The most precious things which man truly needs are pure air to breathe, pure water to drink, and a patch of earth to live upon. These are man's birthright. God grants them unstintedly; but man's own fellow-beings would not permit him a free use of them. Hence the need has arisen for fortified dwelling in congested areas. Hence all disease and concomitant evils. If man's needs were simple, his wants few, and his social laws less complicated, there would be an end to all strife and discord, and peace and order would prevail all over the world. But thanks to the multiplicity of their interests and unchecked ambition, this world has become a veritable hell for most men. Oh, if any other Messiah or a Nanak came and tore up the web of hypocrisy which men have woven, and under the cover of which they commit unnamable atrocities, nay, glory in them ! Men might hold up their heads only when militarism becomes a thing of the past, when they look upon all their fellow-men as brothers and all women as sisters, when they share what they have with others, when they all work for common weal and realize their interdependence upon one another, and understand that their own healthful and blissful living depends on the healthful and blissful living of each and every member of society. And this is only possible when man-made laws give place to God-made laws. Till that era dawns, the history of man will continue to be an endless tale of woe.

CHAPTER XIX

BABA DIP SINGH

This martyr received martyrdom in an attempt to rescue the Temple at Amritsar from the hands of the Turks.

When Mir Mannu of cursed memory, Governor of Lahore, died of a fall from his horse, and Mir Mohammad who had taken hundreds of Sikh ladies into custody and caused them terrible sufferings, was caught and slain, while flying to Lahore, and cremated, Ahmad Shah Abdali appointed Jahan Khan Subah of Lahore, with orders to extirpate the Khalsa root and branch. Jahan Khan's men roamed about the villages in search of the Khalsa and spread havoc throughout the land. The Khalsa left their homes and took shelter in far-off jungles. Jahan Khan made Amritsar his headquarters. To flout the sentiments of the Khalsa, he demolished their temple and had the Tank of Immortality filled up. The report of this sacrilege reached far and near and infuriated the believers. The Khalsa emerged from their retreats in the Malwa and marched to Amritsar under the leadership of Baba Dip Singh. At Tarn Taran they halted to rest a while and to pray, at the Gurdwara there, for strength to chastise their savage foe, and prevent his incursions into their territory. On their wrists they wore festal ribbons and on their heads they put saffron-sprinkled turbans, as if they were out to fight for and win brides for themselves. Jahan Khan was apprised of the march. With a force of of 20,000 men he met the Khalsa, 6,000 strong, at the village Golerwal, about 5 miles from Amritsar. The fight, as may be imagined, was sanguinary. Jahan Khan, the Pathan Commander, rode on an elephant and was watching the operations. Dayal Singh, a lieutenant of Baba Dip Singh, with a party of 500 companions, cut his way to where the Commander Jahan Khan was standing. The steed under him made one brave spring and enabled him to chop off Jahan Khan's head as if it was that of a carrot. Upon this Jahan Khan's second-in-command, with a number of his officers, made a rush at Dayal Singh. The struggle was severe. Both sides lost heavily. But it pleased the great God to grant the Khalsa an advantage over the enemy, who fled in disorder pursued by the Khalsa soldiery. Arrived at Ramsar, in the city, they rallied and gave another battle. The result was a terrible massacre. Jamal Shah, one of the commanders, challenged Baba Dip Singh to a hand to hand fight. The challenge was accepted. Both fought bravely, till they were fatally wounded. It is said that the headless body of Baba Dip Singh went on for some time committing havoc among the ranks of the enemy. Dharm Singh, Khem Singh, Man Singh and Ram Singh, besides other Sikh soldiers, rushed into the thick of the fight and wrought terrible slaughter, before they were cut down themselves (1760 A.D.) Their admirers raised monuments to their honour which stand to this day The streets were filled with heaps of the slain and blood flowed in the drains. The cries of "Sat Sri Akal !" and "Ya Ali ! Ya

Ali !" reverberated throughout the city. The struggle was the keenest at the place now known as Guru-ka-Bagh. The Khalsa had mustered there in great force to offer battle to the Pathans. Sardar Hira Singh put Sabar Ali Khan, one of the commanders, to death. Zabardast Khan, another commander, stepped forward to deal Sabar Ali's assailant a blow; but before he could achieve anything he was felled down by Balwant Singh, one of the Sardars. Zabardast's brother, Rustam Ali Khan advanced against Balwant Singh and his men. The engagement was very sharp and both the combatants fell in the battle. The Sikhs fought like lions. With the fall of Zabardast, the Pathans fled for their lives and victory attended the arms of the Khalsa. The retreating Pathans were pursued, till they reached Atari. Large quantities of ammunition and provisions fell into the hands of the Khalsa.

A Gurdwara stands on the banks of Babek Sar in memory of Sardar Dharm Singh. A Shahid Ganj, near the Akhara of Magni Ram; commemorates the martyrdoms of Sardars Kaur

Singh, Manna Singh, Sant Singh and others. Sardar Ram Singh has a memorial in Katra Ram Garhian.

CHAPTER XX

BABA GURBAKSH SINGH

This martyr received martyrdom in 1760 A.D. He was a resident of Seel, a village near Khem Karan in the District of Lahore. He was baptized into the Khalsa faith by Bhai Mani Singh and, thenceforth, he devoted himself to the service of the Panth. He was one of the brave lieutenants who had given a good account of their valour in the battle of Ramsar in the city of Amritsar, where Baba Dip Singh had received martyrdom. He lived for the most part at Anandpur and derived inspiration from its sacred associations. When the Mahrattas turned out Najib-ud-Daulah, the Agent of Ahmad Shah Abdali in Delhi, the latter, enranged at their audacity, led a large army against them, and reached Delhi unopposed. The Khalsa were not then strong enough to meet an enemy of

Abdali's intrepidity in the open field. They had, hitherto, contented themselves with night attacks on their foes, whenever an opportunity presented itself. Abdali had with him a huge army of well-disciplined and well-equipped men, and a host of irregulars, whom he left free to rob and plunder the places through which they passed. In times of war, men, everywhere, give loose reins to their passions and commit all sorts of excesses. Abdali's men were particulary cruel and ferocious,—absolute savages, who took delight in rapine and plunder. At the report of their approach, men fled for their lives and left their homes and belongings at the mercy of their predatory foes, who appropriated to themselves whatever they could lay their hands upon, put all old men and women to the sword and carried young people into slavery. Their chief pastime was the plunder and devastation of Hindu and Sikh temples, in which they were not unoften assisted by their co-religionists of the country. The Temple at Amritsar sacred to the memory of Guru Ram Das, shared the same fate. When the news of the desecration reached Anandpur, the Khalsa there were filled with rage. Baba Gurbaksh Singh, then vowed to march to Amritsar and wreak vengeance on the foe. A small party of intrepid young men volunteered to accompany him. Their way lay through an inhospitable country; but the gallant crusaders easily got over all obstacles and reached their destination in due time. The local Sikhs acclaimed them. The invaders were turned out and those who opposed were given short shrift. The temple was soon placed in a state of repairs and regular worship was restored. The Lahore Government was soon informed of the *Coup a'etat.* It lost no time in sending a small expeditionary force under commanders Khan Jahan and Buland Khan. There was a sharp action in the vicinity of Akal Bungah, in which Baba Gurbaksh Singh received a mortal wound and fell. Round his corpse there was a hand to hand fight till, at last, the Baba's comrades were slain to a man. They were cremated, then and there, and the place was named Shahid Ganj. On the 9th of the lunar month, a regular service is held at the seat of his martyrdom. At Anandpur a temple was erected in his honour by Sardar Suba Singh. The Mussalmans returned victorious and they again adopted all kinds of repressive measures, making no effort at reconciliation. The result was the slow but sure alienation of the sympathies of the Khalsa who grew the more, the more they were destroyed.

CHAPTEK XXI

A PEEP INTO THE HISTORY OF KASUR

In 1760 A.D., a number of Brahmans waited upon the Khalsa in their abode in the jungles, and appealed to them for help in the rescue of their ladies, who had been carried off by the Pathans of Kasur. The pathetic tale drew tears from the eyes of the hearers. Nothing appealed to the chivalrous instinct of the Khalsa more than such a work. Forthwith, preparations were made for an attack on Kasur. This was a Pathan colony of seven settlements. On account of its close proximity to Lahore, and the influence of its notables at the Lahore Court, it was a place of importance, second only to Lahore. Its people had grown immensely rich, during Mussalman rule, partly on account of the positions which the scions of its various families held in the State, but chiefly on acccount of th incursions of its chieftains into the remote parts of the Empire, from where they invariably brought immense booty. Stories of its fabulous wealth and of the escapades and flirtations of the amorous Pathan youth and damsels, formed the burthen of the songs of the national bards. Indeed, if tradition is to be believed, this town was a more recent copy of the Sodom and Gomorrah of the Christian Bible. Inebriated with uncontrolled power, and, immune from the constant inroads of the plundering hordes of the north-west border, who came with the ferocity of a tornado and went back with the swiftness of a hurricane, on account of its comparatively safe distance from the grand trunk road from Kabul to Delhi. its population seems to have lost all respect for God and goodness, and it was only meet and proper that its fate should have borne resemblance to that of the afore-mentioned towns of which nothing but a memory now survives. Fire and brimstone have not rained on Kasur; neither has it been swallowed up by the sea, through a cataclysmal change, but the seven islets on which it so proudly stood, are now represented by as many sand-hills, bearing on their surface the marks of devastation, that the offended Deity seems to have ordained through its chosen instruments. The modern townlet of this name has been built on the ancient ruins, and its prosperity is due to its being a junction station and its possessing a grain market, which are the results of Pax Britannia.

It does not, therefore, require much effort to imagine that the affair of the forcible removal of the Brahman girls, above alluded to, could not have been an isolated instance of the kind. There was no Hindu potentate to redress such complaints, and the Mussalman rulers generally turned deaf ear when appealed to. Hence the complaint to the Khalsa.

One fine day, when it was blazing hot, and the people had retired for rest into the inner most closets of their houses the cries of "Sat-Sri Akal", and the clashing of the Khalsa scimitars roused the inhabitants from their pleasant slumbers. The Khalsa band had surrounded the mansions of the great Khans and Nawabs. The Brahman girls were rescued and restored to their guardians. Any number of lewd and profligate Pathans, in the arms of their paramours, were dragged from their beds and were then and there put to the sword. Many Hindu and Sikh girls that had been abducted and seduced, were liberated and sent back to their rightful guardians. The gold and jewellery that fell into the hands of the Khalsa, were freely distributed among the poor and the oppressed, and the men who had interfered with the freedom of worship of the Sikhs and the Hindus, and had otherwise, taken a prominent share in molesting them, received condign punishment.

The news of this splendid ruse nonplussed the enemy throughout the province, and filled them with mortification and chagrin. The engines of oppression were again set in motion but by this time all the power of the local Turk ruling classes had spent itself. Everywhere the Khalsa raised their heads, and many Turk nobles and their willing Hindu agents like Shiv

Dayal, a follower of Jafar Khan of Gurdaspur, were brought to their knees Mohammad Khan Nawab of Pasrur, and Nur Din of Kalanaur shared a similar fate. The enraged Khalsa did not spare even Lahore which was invaded in broad daylight. The Turk oppressors who could be got hold of in the city, were made to taste the sword of the Khalsa. Hamid Khan the Subah, saved his life by hiding in the Fort.

CHAPTER XXII

THE GREAT HOLOCAUST–GOLDEN TEMPLE DEMOLISHED

In a fit of despair, the Punjab Moslems and their Hindu abettors like Akil Das, an Udasi Mahant of Jandiala appealed for help to Ahmad Shah Abdali who started on his eighth invasion of India, in the early part of 1762 A.D., with 40,000 cavalry and innumerable foot-soldiers, belonging to the fighting Pathan clans of the North-West Frontier. When this became known, all well-to-do Hindus took shelter in out-of-the-way places. The Khalsa thought it prudent to take their wives and children with them and migrate to Malwa. But they had hardly crossed the Sutlej when, in response to the Abdali's call, the Lahore army, together with the contingents brought by Zain Khan,

Subah of Sirhind, Bhikhan Khan of Maler Kotla, Wazir Hussain of Rai Kot, and the lesser Moslem and anti-Khalsa Hindu chiefs, overtook them near Jagraon. Though taken by surprise, the Khalsa did not lose heart. Old men, women and children, with such valuables as they possessed, among which were the Granth compiled by the tenth Guru, and such other literary treasures as had been rescued from the predatory Hindu Hill Rajas and their Moslem allies, after their treacherous attack on the Khalsa garrison of Anandpur, were sent forward under the escort of a few veteran warriors. The rest prepared to give battle to the enemy, and rendered a good account of themselves, while they still continued their march with their ranks unbroken. Next morning Abdali himself overtook them on the plains of Raipur Gujarwal. The battle now assumed serious proportions. The struggle was an unequal one. The Abdali's men, 150,000 strong, leaving aside the local levies from the Punjab were all picked soldiers, well-equipped and well-supplied with provisions.

The case with the Khalsa was quite different. Being forced to live in desert wastes and wild forests, and deprived of the amenities of civilized life, they could command only the crudest of weapons. Moreover, they were weighted down by their families and were thus seriously handicapped. But they were not men who would give their lives cheaply. They determined to die to a man, then and there, but not till they had made short work of the savage foe, and rendered it impossible for him to think of molesting the Khalsa again. In this aim they were eminently successful. It is true that all the migrating Khalsa, about 30,000 in number, were almost decimated. Their wives and children, who had been sent ahead, were waylaid and cruelly butchered, and their valuables, including the scriptures and literary treasures, were carried off, but the loss of the Abdali both in officers and men, was not inconsiderable. For miles round the corpses of the Ghilzai lay unburied in heaps, to become the food of kites and vultures, wolves and jackals. Sad and dejected, he returned to Manjha. The town of

Amritsar, on account of its sacred tank that gave it its name, was the chief rendezvous of the Khalsa. He caused the tank to be filled up, and the Golden Temple standing in its middle to be blown up by gun-powder, evidently under the impression that with the disappearance of their sacred edifice, the power of the Khalsa would vanish from the earth. But in this belief he was seriously mistaken.

The Khalsa had not till now, desecrated the sacred places of the Turks. The blowing up of the Amritsar Temple roused their worst passions and, though, be it said to their credit, they did not copy the ways of the Turk Huns in their entirety, in this there is no doubt that the vengeance they wreaked was a terrible one.

While the Abdali was engaged in blowing up the Temple, a missile from the blown-up edifice is said to have struck his knee, upon which he ordered a hasty retreat from the scene of his savagery. The festering wound brought on a malady which ate into his vitals. Over and above this, came the reports of the plight of Kabuli Mal whom he had appointed Governor of Lahore,[1] and of the occupation of Lahore, nay, of the whole Province, by the redoubtable Khalsa. These had a very disquieting effect on his mind. He essayed once more, and for the last time, to crush the Khalsa; but like the last flicker of a dying flame, his military genius failed him. On the plains of the "Bara Ghallu Ghara' he met the Khalsa forces again, but they vanished from his sight like a cloud. Marching eastward, he met Raja Amar Singh Phul, grandson of the redoubtable Raja Ala Singh towards whom he adopted a conciliatory policy by granting him the title of "Raja-i-Rajgan"; but conciliation or no conciliation, he was defeated in his attempt to get rid this nest of hornets, as he called the Khalsa. Like veritable

1. 'The Shah made a Hindu named Kabuli Mal, his Governor at Lahore, and then hastened towards Kandhar to suppress an insurrection in that distant quarter; but he first gratified his own resentment and indulged the savage bigotry of his followers by destroying the renowned Temple of Amritsar, by polluting the pool with slaughtered cows, by encasing numerous pyramid with the heads of decapitated Sikhs, and by cleansing the walls of desecrated mosques with the blood of his infidel enemies"—History of the Sikhs, by D. Cunningham, 1853 edition p. 101.

hornets, they followed him till he was sick unto death. He died soon after, leaving a legacy of crime, a crop of Dragons' Teeth, which only ended in the total extinction of his house before two generations were over. Even his name would have been forgotten, but for the epigram which got current in his day and is still remembered: —"*Jo khada so lahe da, rahinda Ahmad Shahe da, i.e.,*" whatever is eaten is ours, the rest belongs to Ahmad Shah

One reads with breathless astonishment the enconiums bestowed even on a creature like this. Says Sayed Mohammad Latif (History of the Punjab p. 239):—"He courted the society of learned men and showed the greatest respect to the leaders of religion." This yearning for the society of learned men and of men of religion, had little influence on Ahmad Shah's general conduct. for the same author says further on that "he (Ahmad Shah) often had recourse to fraudulent means and bloodshed, in order to attain his ends, but," adds our author. "we most look to the usages of the times and judge of his conduct by the prevailing customs of contemporary Asiatic monarchs who, we find, employed treachery in all their dealings." Comments are needless.

CHAPTER XXIII

THE REVENGE

The Khalsa rose from their ashes like the proverbial Pheonix, and spread over the country like swarms of locusts. Under their blighting shadow the Turk power lost all vitalising force, and fell like the Lucifer to rise no more. Sirhind was again invaded and destroyed, and its ruler, Zain Khan, fell under the sword of Sardar Jassa Singh Ahluwalia. The Subah's nephew, as well as Yar Mohammad, the commander of the Sirhind army, met the same fate. Their men fled for their lives, leaving Sirhind and its people undefended. Sad, indeed was the plight of Turk residents, who had now to expiate for the excesses of unscrupulous tyrants of their faith who had infuriated the whole Jat population of the country, belonging to the Khalsa faith, against them. The sight of the place reminded the Khalsa of the atrocious deeds of the previous Subahs, especially the bricking up alive of the Princes Zorawar Singh and Fateh Singh, and a high wave of passions surged in their hearts. The infuriated Khalsa soldiery gave no quarter to the fallen foe, and did not rest content till they had razed the whole town to the ground and turned its inhabitants out to shift for themselves as best they might. The village of Muranda, the place of residence of Jani Khan, Mani Khan and Gulsher who, conjointly with Gangu Brahman, had been instrumental in the captivity of Princes Zorawar Singh and Fateh Singh, and their grand mother, Gujri, was again invested and razed to the ground. The unscrupulous Rahmat Ulah and the renegade Diwan Lachhi Ram, Phagwaria, had to pay a heavy penalty for the part they had taken in the unprovoked attack on the Khalsa on their peaceful emigration to Malwa. Bhikhan Khan of Maler Kotla who had interested himself in the recent persecution of the Khalsa, was allowed to escape unpunished. The munition and the provisions that fell into the hands of the Khalsa at these places, enabled them to make a clean sweep of the whole eastern Punjab, as far as Saharanpur, till, overcoming all resistance, they returned home jubilant But they did not remain idle for long. Before another month had passed, they spread over the country again, and took the reins of the Government into their own hands. The Turk rulers fled before them, and those who remained, acknowledged the supremacy of the Khalsa. Taimur, Ahmad Shah's son, abandoned his Satrapy of Lahore and fled to Kabul.

There is nothing which the savage Pathan respects more than savage retaliation. The Khalsa understood this trait of Pathan character and invariably paid him back in his own coin. For the insult offered to the Golden Temple and other connected religious houses in Amritsar, they simply paid the Pathan tit for tat. But though according to Sayed Mohammad Latif, they razed to the ground numerous mosques and compelled "Afghan prisoners, who were in chains, to smear the debris with the blood of hogs," it may be noted with satisfaction, that these retaliatory acts were not accompained by man-slaughter to furnish skulls for raising pyramids, which was the usual pastime of the Pathan.

CHAPTER XXIV

BABA RAM SINGH BEDI

This martyr was the son of the famous Baba Faqir Chand Bedi, The village founded by him in the Sialkot district, known by the name of Kotli Baba Faqir Chand, has grown into an interesting townlet. Tradition credits Baba Faqir Chand with the possession of miraculous powers, for which he was highly venerated by the people. That there was something really great in him, is more than amply borne out by his being blessed with a son in the person of the subject of this narrative. The name of Mir Ahmad Khan,popularly known as Shahanchi Khan, is associated with many an act of atrocity; the mere thought of which makes one shudder with horror. The levity and baseness, which he showed in inventing and practising countless ways of inflicting torture on Khalsa men and women, boys and girls, would shame even the most shameless present-day Pathan assassins, to whom raiding Hindu homes, murdering male immates and outraging or carrying off into captivity young damsels married or unmarried, making their freshly cut-off heads dance on red-hot iron plates, is a mere pastime. He led a party of itinerant Turks, whose sole duty it was to ferret out people of the Khalsa faith, and to put them to death, regardless of sex and age. He had come on such an errand to these parts and had encamped on a mound close to the village of Paropi, some three miles from Kotli. At the news of his arrival, Baba Ram Singh, then a mere callow youth, collected the Khalsa of his village and asked them to die fighting rather than be shot like dogs in the streets, or be hunted and killed like wild beasts. The appeal was successful. A dozen of devoted Sikhs offered to accompany him, wherever he would lead them. As this band proceeded in the direction of the enemy camp, it was joined by more men from the adjoining villages. The enemy had no thought that they would meet with active opposition. Even when they were apprised of the approach of the Khalsa band, they did not show much concern, so low was their opinion of the fighting capacity of the Khalsa. It did not take them long to be disabused of this belief. Baba Ram Singh's party simply wrought havoc in their ranks. There was a terrible carnage, resulting in the total discomfiture of the Turk forces. The Baba ran to and fro making a cleavage right and left, to the wonder and awe of every one, friend or foe. At last he received a mortal blow and fighting to the end (1799 A D.). On the spot where he fell there stands a Gurdwara in his memory. His head was taken to Lahore by the Turks, from whom it was purchased by a devoted follower who cremated it near Masti Gate. A Jagir is attached to this temple and the Bhalla Sahibzadas are in charge of it. Its popularity is, however, waning, for causes which the scope of this narrative does not permit to be discussed here. A relic of the martyr was taken to Peshawar, whe e it was buried near the fort, and a temple was built after the name of the martyr.

This is perhaps one solitary instance of a Bedi Sahibzada receiving martyrdom. Otherwise, the honour of martyrdom has been the proud privilege exclusively of the noble Sodhi Gurus and their descendants and followers.

CHAPTER XXV

DEATH OF SHAHANCHI—AFGHANS DEPART

The Moghal power had long since been destroyed in the Punjab by the incursions of the Pathans and the insurrection of the Khalsa. Now came the turn of the Pathans themselves to go. But the violence with which they struck at the invincible Khalsa, in their last long gasp, before they expired as a superior, political power, was even greater than before. Shah Zaman, the grandson of the Abdali dreamed in vain for the establishment of an Indian empire. As often as he marched out to invade India, an instruction broke out in Afghanistan itself, and he had to hurry back leaving his conquests in India unfinished. He had, however, left his General Ahmad Khan; commonly called Shahnachi Khan: at the head of 7,000 horses to overrun the Punjab and do all he could to extirpate the Khalsa.To all accounts, this man was not less cruel,or less inhuman,than the hated Mannu himself. Like a voracious demon, he stalked over the whole land, now here,now there,carrying fire and sword wherever he went. But the Pathan had now reached the end of his tether. His name had ceased to inspire the awe it had done erstwhile. The Afghan forces under Shahanchi were defeated with great loss near Rohtas,and several thousand beautiful Hindu damsels, whom the miscreant was carrying off to Kabul, were rescued and sent home. In a subsequent action at Gujrat, Shahanchi suffered another defeat, but this did not dispirit him. Rallying his forces again, he attacked the Khalsa army-headquarters near Sialkot, where, in a sanguinary fight, he received a bullet wound and fell with 30,000 of his followers and Mussalman allies of the Sind Sagar and Rachna Doabs. The Khalsa casualties were 8,0.0.

With the death of Shanchi Khan closed the chapter of Moslem persecution of the Khalsa.

Freed from oppression, they started on their new career of power, won by the sacrifice of millions of innocent lives. A holy Christian has said, "the blood of the martyrs is the seed of the church." If this saying was true of Christian peoples, it was equally true of the Khalsa. Who could have dreamed that Nanak's eclectic creed would, in a couple of centuries, become a militant faith ? Who could have imagined that the very son of Guru Arjan Dev, the meekest, sweetest and humblest of men who, like the blessed Christ, laid it down in the Sikh holy book that best punishment that could be meted out to a person who boxed one's ear was to take hold of his feet and kiss them, would, on accession to the *Gadi*, find it necessary to take up the sword and chastise evil-doers ? The fact is that, as the night follows the day, reaction follows action. It is an immutable law of nature, conspicuously exemplified and illustrated by the history of man. As said elsewhere in this book, man everywhere shows himself in his daily life to be more savage than the savage beast of the jungle unless, of course, he is influenced by the cxample and teaching of godly men. Otherwise, perhaps, the only motive that holds him in check, is the fear of being paid back in his own coin. The Khalsa met the cruel Turks on their own ground. The Turks wanted a sabre thrust into their breast, and a sabre thrust they had. According to the creed which the Turks professed, as according to the canons of all other great religions, a sovereign is the shadow of God on earth. The sovereignty of a great country had come into their hands. It ought to have inspired them with a sense of responsibility. It ought to have filled their minds with fear of God and love for their fellow-men. Unfortunately, however, both for themselves and for the subject population whatever of good feelings they had was for men of their own creed. For others they felt no pity or compunction. When on their thrones, they behaved like Pharaohs or Nimrods. The great Nanak truly described Turk regime when he said that it was "a dark age when the sword alone was in display. The rulers were butchers and virtue had taken wings and flown away. In the darkest night of Falsehood, the Moon of Truth was now here visible in the sky."

A more servere inditemant it is difficult to conceive of. When Baba Nanak made these observations,the Turks had just started on their career of conquest. For three centuries more their inglorious sway continued unchecked. Warnings remained unheeded. Besotted profligates, drunk with despotic power, and blind bigots in their mistaken zeal for religion, or for self-aggrandisement, did deeds the mere mention of which would send a shudder into one's frame. Men who wield power, great or small, would do well to remember the Day of Judgment and beware ! for,

> It knows nor wrath nor pardon, utter-true
> Its measures mete, its faultless balance weighs;
> Times are as naught, to-morrow it will judge,
> Or after many days.

CHAPTER XXVI

AURANGZEB AND HIS SUCCESSORS – A STUDY

"Important events," as someone has said, "cast their shadows behind." O, if men could see the results of actions done under the impulse of the moment! Blinded by lust or passion, they do deeds the mere thought of which ought to make them feel, in their calm moments, very small indeed, unless, of course, they are lost to all sense of right or equity. Sometime back, there appeared in an English magazine a lecture on "Man" by Mr. John Asquith, late Prime Minister of England, delivered under the auspices of the Royal Society of Arts, London. Mr. Asquith took great pains to show how noble man was,—noble in his mien, noble and dignified in his erect posture – as compared with his other *confreres* of the mammalian species, who have all to bend their necks as they roam about. And this great compliment the great English statesman paid to his species when the best specimens of his own race were engaged in the dastardly act of man-slaughter in the recent World War with the help of poison gases, of aeroplanes and sea-planes, torpedoes, submarines tanks and other infernal machines. To my mind a man can, when he chooses show himself to be the lowest and meanest of all creatures. The wolf and the tiger conceal themselves during the day, and only come out during the night in search of their food, when they attack weaker animals. Even the cobra does not attack unless he is assailed, or fears that his own life is in endanger. But there is no fixed time of attack for man, and there is no limit to his appetite. The paradise of which the scriptures of all religions give such graphic accounts, and for which any number of innocent people long with such avidity, is perhaps beyond the reach of the living. But the hell of which we read so much is here on this globe of ours, made not by a Satan, who is only a creature of the imagination of some good people, but by human fiends, who, in the shape of man, are bigger Devils than the Devil himself. If the Evil One really exists, and can take human shape and visit human abodes, there is no doubt that even he would feel ashamed to be regarded as the prototype of a being who is said to have been made in God's own image.

In the foregoing pages, an attempt has been made to portray the Turk bigots as they showed themselves in their dealings with the less virile Hindus and with the Sikhs. The extracts that follow will show how the tyrants treated their own relatives and co-religionists. It will be amusing to note that the free-booter, Ahmad Shah, like his prototype Mahmud of Ghazni, believed he was promoting the cause of religion by his campaigns of murder and plunder, when, as a matter of fact, he was pandering to his own greed and avarice. Not less amusing will be the perusal of the passage describing the crocodile tears of Aurangzeb when his brother, Dara Shikoh's head was brought to him as if Dara had died a natural death, and Aurangzeb himself was in no way responsible for his premature end. The astonishment is heightened when it is borne in mind that Aurangzeb, who is admitted to have been a highly cultured, wide-awake and shrewd monarch, failed to see that his own long reign of atrocious deeds fomented discord, created inveterate hatred of the very name of Turk and provoked the Sikhs and the Hindus to revolt, and that it was he himself who, all the while, was engaged in striking at the very root of his empire fondly believing that he was but nurturing the tree while he was actually cutting it. "The third son, Aurangzeb," says Sayed Mohammad Latif, "was able, cautious, ambitious and designing. He held religious discourses with pious men and affected to be more ambitions of obtaining a reputation as a faqir, or saint, than as a great lord. He spent his time mostly in meditation, prayer and reading the Koran, and went even so far as to pretend that he subsisted on the earnings of his manual labour. He subsequently declared his resolution of renouncing the world and proceeding on a pilgrimage to Mecca; but was deterred from doing so by his father, who was quite unconscious that the crafty young man would afterwards prove himself a dangerous opponent. Aurangzeb concealed his ambitious designs behind the veil of religion." (History of the Punjab, p. 17.)

Further on we read: "He feigned to resign in favour of Murad, telling him in his letters, 'I have not the slightest wish to take any part in the government of this deceitful and unstable world; my only desire is that I may make a pilgrimage to the temple of God.' These professions induced Murad to join his forces to those of the dissembler and the confederate armies put Dara and Shujah to flight Aurangzeb, by a stratagem, then made Murad prisoner, and removed him to the fort of Gwalior, where he was executed." (*Ibid*, p. 172.) "Dara was condemned to death by the lawyers, and the sentence was, with apparent reluctance confirmed by Aurangzeb. A personal enemy was directed to carry out the sentence ...... His body was exhibited on an elephant to the populace; while his head was brought to Aurangzeb, who had it wiped and washed in his presence, and being satisfied of its identity, shed tears" (*Ibid*, p. 173.)

"Aurangeb had resolved that the belief in one God and the Prophet should be not the prevailing, but the only religion of the empire of Hindustan. He issued mandates to the Viceroys and Governors of Provinces to destroy pagodas and idols throughout his dominions. The Emperor appointed Mullahs with a party of horses attached to each, to check all ostentatious display of idol-worship, and sometimes afterwards he forbade fairs on Hindu festivals and issued a circular to all Governors and men in authority, prohibiting the employment of Hindus in the offices of State. The Emperor issued an edict prohibiting Hindus from being carried in palanquins or riding on Arab horses. All servants of State were ordered to embrace the Mohammadan religion under pain of dismissal, and those who refuse were deprived of their posts. A large number of Yogis, Sanyasis and other religious men were driven out of the

King's dominions. In the twenty-second year of his reign he renewed the Jaziah, or poll-tax on Hindus, throughout his dominions. The Hindus of Delhi gathered in large numbers beneath the Jharoka, window, on the banks of the river, and implored. His Majesty to remit the obnoxious tax, but the Emperor was inexorable. The Hindus adopted the expedient of closing the shops in the city and all business came to a stand-still. They thronged the bazar from the palace to the Grand Mosque, on a Friday, with the object of seeking relief. The crowd increased every moment and the King's equippage was interrupted at every step. He stopped for a while to hear them; but the multitude held their ground. At length under orders from the Emperor, war elephants were directed against the mob and the retinue forcing the way through, numbers were trodden to death by horses and elephants. (*Ibid*, pp. 176 —177).

"Some questions of etiquette which arose, created such a difference between the King of Delhi and Shah Abbas of Persia, that under the orders of His Persian Majesty, the beard of the Indian envoy was set on fire by a page. The Emperor's wrath on the return of the beardless envoy knew no bounds. He reproached him bitterly for not having stabbed the Shah to the heart and executed him the same day by having him bitten by venomous snake." (*Ibid*, p. 177).

"The Satnamis, a sect of Hindu devotees, had risen in revolt and committed great excesses. The royal troops defeated the insurgents and massacred in cold blood the male inhabitants of the localities where the insurrection had broken out. Women and children were seized and sold as slaves.". (*Ibid*, p. 177.)

"The Emperor recalled Amin Khan and appointed one Kasim Khan in his place. Kasim Khan an experienced chief and won the hearts of Afghans by his seeming courtesy and friendship. He entertained the Afghans at a great banquet held at Peshawar, in honour of the circumcision ceremony of his son, and gave them splendid feast in the grand square of the city, Horse-racing, elephant-fights, games and exhibitions were the order of the day. In the midst of these rejoicings, Kasim Khan suddenly left the assembly, which was a signal for a massacre. Bodies of armed men who had been concealed in the neighbouring houses, poured volleys of musketry on the Afghan guests, who had attended the feast without a suspicion of treachery. There was a general massacre of Afghans and it spread consternation throughout Kabul. The Afghans were paralysed and gave no further trouble for the rest of Aurangzeb's reign." (*Ibid*, p. 178).

It is a pity that Mohammadan writers have not felt ashamed of giving to such a monster the credit of being a rigid Mussalman. He himself was, however, more honest in describing the innermost working of his mind than his so-called biographers. This is how he wrote to Kam Baksh, his youngest son from his Georgian wife; towards the close of his impious career:- "I come a stranger into this world and a stranger I depart I know nothing of myself —what I am and for what I am destined. My back is bent with weakness and my feet have lost the power of motion. The breath which rose is gone and has left not even hope behind it." (*Ibid* p. 178).

"Aurangzeb's attachment to Mohammadanism seems to have been sincere, but his bigotry and intolerance towards Hindus revived religious animosities between the various classes of population, and the disintegration of races to which his hypocrisy gave rise, paved the way for the speedy dismemberment of the once powerful Moghal monarchy in India." (*Ibid*, p. 172.)

"Aurangzeb sent a European physician to treat the old king. The name of this physician is not stated, but he had been employed in more than one work of poisoning and had been advanced to high offices in the State. The death of Shah Jahan was soon announced. The suspicion was never removed that the aged king had been removed by poisoning." (*Ibid*, p. 174.)

Those good people who so glibly talk and write of Guru Nanak's spirituality, and take exception to Guru Gobind Singh's drawing the sword to punish the prepetrators of wrong, will do well to read the above blood-curdling details and honestly say if they would tolerate such atrocities. They might do so; but that would be principally due to their lack of all sense of honour and self-respect, and to rank moral cowardice, which they, in vain, cleverly try to conceal from public gaze. Even the dog and the pig manage to eke out their existence. To exist merely in peace and quiet, without feeling for one's fellow-men and sharing their grief and sorrow, does not befit the animal who is said to have been made in the "image of God," and who certainly believes himself to be the noblest of created beings. "Dost thou remember" says the blessed Sadi, "that when thou wast born, thou criedst but other people rejoiced. Die so that at the time of thy death, thou shouldst rejoice and others cry." Will men follow this great teacher ?

The fact is that the Moghal Empire had run out its course. It died with Aurangzeb, and the puppet rulers who succeeded him one after the other shamelessly, gambled with its corpse. They were mostly a besotted, devil-may-care sort of remorseless persons whom nothing could shame. This is what an historian says about them :—"The first act of the new Emperor (Jahander Shah) after coming to power was to pollute his hands with the blood of the princes royal, a crime which had become characteristic of the race of Timur. Jahandar Shah was a weak and indolent prince, effeminate, licentious and fond of ease. The Emperor became so dead to all feelings of shame that in passing through the streets he seized the wives and daughters of the lowest tradesmen." (History of the Punjab by Mohammad Latif, pp. 185-186.)

"He (Farrukh Syar) commenced the reign of terror during which period he spared none, whether Hindu or Moslem. He was weak and timid, destitute of morals and capacity, and lavished favours on low people. (*Ibid*, pp. 187–188.)

Farrukh Syar did not take long to meet Divine Justice. He fell out with the Sayed brothers, who easily dragged him out of the recesses of his seraglio and deprived him of sight. "After suffering all the agonies of a lingering death, he was plunged into a solitary cell. A leathern thong was strained round his neck. The prince tried to keep it off his neck by holding it with both his hands, and struggled desperately with his hands and feet. But there was no escape, and the unhappy prince had the misfortune of suffering dint of blows in addition to a painful death caused by a dagger.'' (*Ibid*. p. 189.)

CHAPTER XXVII

THE KHALSA EMERGES TRIUMPHANT

Guru Govind Singh had vowed that his sparrows should challenge hawks to a fight and kill them. This vow he saw fulfilled in his own life-time, short though unfortunately it was. Under the influence of his baptism, men worked wonders. Every hamlet that harboured the Khalsa, sent forth never-ending streams of chivalrous young men ready to do and dare for the honour of their faith and the defence of their homes. Princes quailed on their thrones at the very mention of their name, and hosts of trained, well-armed men flew before them as does the straw before a wind. It was this spirit that had led the Khalsa to fall upon the Turk hordes under the great free-booters, Nadir Shah and Ahmad Shah on their way back from Delhi, made them taste of their steel and wrested from

Nadir the well-known remark that these men would soon become kings It was the same spirit again, which rendered abortive the repeated attacks of Ahmad Shah, his son and grandson, and put an end to their schemes of founding an Afghan empire in India. Nadir Shah had to lose a good portion of the fabulous wealth, which he had carried from the Imperial Delhi, and Ahmad Shah Abdali was not less unlucky. Each and every time that he passedd through the central districts of the Punjab, he had to part with much of the treasure and valuables which he had brought from the sack of Delhi and other places in Hindustan. Once he was marching to Kabul with 2,000 captives consisting of young Hindu boys and girls. When the Pathan army had crossed the Jullandhar Doab with the prisoners, the Khalsa fell upon them and killed 2,000 of the enemy together with their leader, Bakhshi Abdul Rahim Khan. The Hindu ladies and children were rescued and sent to their guardians, whom centuries of subjection had completely emasculated, and who could only give vent to their grief by cries and lamentations, not unlike goats and sheep, as they are led bleating to the shambles. The Abdali was, of course, deeply incensed at this affront, and the cruel deeds he did to avenge this wrong, only served to demoralise his own men and his co-religionists in the Punjab, with the result that Pathan name ceased to inspire dread, and the victorious Khalsa carried war even into the mountain fastnesses of Afghanistan, where the Khalsa name is still held in awe.

Hindus all over India can easily imagine what their lot would have been if the Khalsa had not borne the brunt of Pathan invasions as gate-keepers of India, and made future incursions from the north-west a remote possibility. The invaders came and went back unchecked. A great civilisation, conceived in time immemorial, and nurtured by ages of strenuous research and culture, was ruthlessly destroyed by hosts of savages. Being a resident of that part of the country which received the brunt of the foreign attacks, the writer has, not unoften, come across charred remains of towns, with markets elegantly designed, and with places of worship built in a style which betokens a high standard of artistic taste, and containing in their niches numerous images, large and small, of the great Buddha, seated in meditative posture, and lending solemnity and purity to the grandeur and charm of the surrounding scenery, which Dame Nature seems to have been at great pains to design and to execute.[1] He has wondered and marvelled at the Sylvan God laying out, in the neighbourhood, vast fields of emerald, stretching for miles around, interspersed with small detached hillocks, the heights of which eternally expose to view floods of light reflected from the shingled beds of numerous rillets and torrents, as they glide along, singing merrily. And he has noticed with indignation Gujjar and Gakhar lads stolidly grazing their herds over hallowed places, from which, centuries ago, men communed with the Sun and the Moon, and whom the carnalities of this sensual world failed to tempt and debase.

This work of vandalism and cruelty was

---

1. Taxila, of which the ruins have been dug up near Rawal Pindi.

undoubtedly of the free-booters who, under the banner of Islam, carried fire and sword wherever they went, to prepare the ground for their new-fangled doctrines. How exacting the Semitic God is, is not unknown to the readers of the Jewish Bible and the Koran. He would be content with nothing short of complete surrender. Our ancestors were not prepared to go to this length, and for this refractoriness they had to pay dearly by the forfeiture of their very ives, and not a vestige of their glory remains in this part of the country. Even their memory would not have been rescued from oblivion, had it not been for the devotion of Buddhist pilgrims, who made it possible for the British Government to sanction an outlay of expenditure for the necessary excavations, and for the preservation of the monuments discovered. These remarks apply equally to the whole North-west Frontier, from the South-western corner of Sindh to the North-western boundaries of Chitral and Kashmere, which are full of *Thehs*,—heads of debris of ruined towns and villages, all telling their blood-written tale. Taxila offered resistance but this was courting extinction. Later, Jai Pal, the Hindu king of Lahore, manfully opposed Moslem aggression, and not being able to put up with the ignominy of a heavy defeat, he burnt himself on the funeral pyre. Our men have left no account of what happened to them, during these days of dire distress, but the savage perpetrators of these atrocities themselves boastfully mention in their memoirs what havoc they wrought. From Mahmud of Ghazni down to Timur, Babar and Nadir Shah, all vain gloriously say that the deeds of rapine, murder and plunder with which their accursed memory is associated, were done not in their own interests, but in the name of their religion What portions of the plunder went to their own share, how many Hindu women and children they carried off into captivity, they do not say. But in this there is no doubt that the Indian Mussalmans, forgetting how cruel these invaders were, and that when their own selfish ends had to be served and their brutal passions to be satisfied, they made no distinction between friend and foe, Moslem and non-Moslem, actually acclaimed them as their deliverers. Says Sayed Mohammad Latif .— 'Mohammadans looked upon him(Shah Zaman, grandson of Ahmad Shah Abdali) as the champion of their faith and the deliverer of their country.The leading Mohammadans of the Punjab, Jalal Bhatti,Nizam-ud-Din Khan of Kasur, and others joined him...Encouragements were held out to the Shah by a refugee Prince of Delhi and Sultan...Intrigues were set on foot in many parts of India to assist the king with the object of eventually restoring the house of Timur to power. The weakness of the Maharattas...induced every able-bodied Mohammadan in Hindustan to arm in the defence of his religion and country. ...The Rohillas, too, were armed *cap-a-pie* and determined to assist the Shah in his endeavour to conquer India; while even in the Deccan the advent of the royal hero was hopefully and anxiously awaited by every Mohammadan. How visionary these hopes were appeared soon after. Intelligence was received of the rebellion of the Shah's brother,

Prince Mahmud, at Herat, and he was compelled forthwith to retrace his steps to Kabul." (History of the Punjab, 302).

But God had ordained otherwise. The Khalsa had already taken possession of Lahore, a consummation which a Mussalman historian commemorated by the chronogram 'Jahane kharab shud' [1]—a world was devastated,—an expression which truly indicates the Mussalman attitude towards Sikh supremacy. When Shah Zaman came for the third time, the Khalsa chiefs vacated Lahore temporarily, but they re-occupied it as soon as his back was turned. From this time forward it remained in their possession, until the government of the country passed into the hands of the East Indian Company.

Thus within less than a hundred years of the ascension of Guru Govind Singh, the Khalsa became the paramount power in their own land and the Turks lay prostrate at their feet. In the whole range of history, there is not another example of a people so suddenly lifted from a

1. Corresponding to Hijra 1181 or 1764 A.D.

position of abject subjection to that of complete supremacy. And this remarkable upheaval was due not to any unexplainable occult cause, but to the immense sacrifices made by the Khalsa in the effort to gain freedom. Their orders were, "Put your heads on the palms of your hands and come unto me." This they vied with one another in doing. With one weapon, faith in God and the Guru, they marched on their career of conquest and in the end became absolute masters. According to Bhai Gyan Singh, author of the Panth Prakash, Nawab Zakriya Khan, truly described the character of the Khalsa of his time when, in reply to Nadir Shah's query, he reported that the homes of the Khalsa were on the saddle, that they lived on leaves and the bark of trees, that roasted gram they prized as almonds and goat's meat they called 'Maha Prasad'— the daintiest dish, that grown-up men from all castes and grades of the Hindus were received into the brotherhood, from which time forward they believed only in one God, that they were brothers to one another eating from one common dish and drinking from one common cup, that they believed themselves to be God's chosen people, especially appointed to establish His Kingdom on earth, and that after they had taken the *Amrita* (baptism), they really believed that they had become immortal. In this there is no doubt that they had absolutely no fear of death. Each Khalsa regarded himself as equal to a lac and a quarter of other people. A batch of twenty men would face thousands of the enemy When they once made up their mind to do a thing, nothing would turn them from their purpose. At the command of their Guru they would jump into fire or water. The more they were killed, the more they flourished. They wore a bracelet of steel round their wrists and a quoit of the same metal on their heads. They were always armed with a sword. In fact steel was their God and they worshipped it as such. Silver and gold did not tempt them. When a treasure came into their hands, they distributed it among the community. They had only one *kachha* (a knicker) to cover their nakedness, and one small turban to cover their heads. The naked earth served them for their beds, on which they slept the most refreshing sleep, and so forth. This unstinted praise from an implacable foe surprised even the brave Nadir Shah, who exclaimed that, if only half of what the Khan Bahadur had said was true, the day was not distant when the Khalsa would become the masters of their country. That he prognosticated aright is amply borne out by history.

CHAPTER XXVIII

GURU GOVIND SINGH'S COSMOPOLITAN IDEAL

If the followers of Baba Nanak, whom both the Sikhs and Mussalmans acknowledged as their Pir, their teacher and guide, and still do so, signally failed in obtaining a friendly regard from their Mussalmans countrymen, who have invariably sided with their foreign co-religionists, where is the guarantee or likelihood of the reality or the permanence of the Hindu-Moslem *entente* or of a united India ? Such a consummation is impossible, unless, of course, there is a radical change in the mentality of the various communities that inhabit the country. The change has been clearly indicated by the great Guru Govind Singh. "Temples and *Masjids*," says he, "are one and the same thing;

Puja and *Namaz* are the same. Men are alike, though they might appear different. Devas, Adevas, Yakshyas, Gandharvas, Turks, Hindus, are so called by virtue of the conditions that prevail in the various lands and regions they inhabit. All are alike in the matter of their eyes and ears, their frames and their build. They are all made of earth, air, fire and water. They have the same common Creator. The Puranas and the Koran speak of the same Divine Being. All are of the same form and are made by One and the same Being. (Akal Ustat). The Guru expatiates further on this theme in a language the beauty of which it is impossible to bring out in a translation.The foregoing excerpt, however, is enough to show the cosmopolitan character of his belief and teaching. It is true he founded a separate sect, gave it a separate organization and made it a distinct self-contained, self-centred entity. But nowhere does he say that the great God is partial to the Khalsa alone, or that there need be any antagonism between the Khalsa and the Mussalmans, or for the matter of that, between any two peoples as a result of theological differences. He definitely and distinctly says that "the wealth and estates of all those who meditate on the Divine Name bud forth like the rose and flourish." So according to Guru Govind Singh, all Theistic people, despite their differences of opinion, from one common church. Such a creed, whatever the name it might bear, can alone bring all people on one common platform.

But he must be an exceedingly bold man who will say that the millennial conditions, which the Guru foreshadowed for the establishment of a united cosmopolitan church, have ever obtained, or that there is any near prospect of their obtaining to any appreciable extent. The Indian Mussalmans look up to Turkey and Arabia, more than to India. Their ideal is Pan-Islamism, and until and unless they come to regard religion as a matter of private concern as indeed it ought to be the idea of a united India nation is merely chimerical. An d so long as this is so, the subordination of communal interests to any utopian scheme of 'liberty' equality, and fraternity,' will be nothing short of national suicide.

In the times to which the events recorded in this narrative relate, the Turks were far from being well organized. On the contrary, they were extremely clannish—a fact which is amply borne out by the many wars they waged against one another. This has now completely changed. The new gospel of Pan-Islamism has united Moslems all over the world, as they never were before, and has made it possible for Turkey to regain the supremacy which she had lost as a result of the World War. Not only this, the Young Turk is now in a position to dictate terms to the Great Powers of Europe combined. All her former barbarities have been forgotten, and Turkey is now acknowledged as a civilised nation among the civilised peoples of Europe and America. The Moslems are even now killing and deporting hundreds of thousands of Jews and Chistians of various nationalities from the lands they have re-occupied, and are outraging their women. What they will do to Hindus and Sikhs when the time comes for the British to leave the control of India, can be better imagined than described. It is unquestionably a beautiful idea to unite Indians of all races and creeds into one homogenous people, but in order that this unity may be something organically sound, it is absolutely necessary that the Hindus and Sikhs, the inheritors of the Indo-Aryan civilisation, should set their own households in order by imbibing the principles preached by Guru Govind Singh, which are bound to rejuvenate them and wrest respect for them from their compeers, whether of their own race or of foreign extraction.